Once Upon a Chair

Design Beyond the Icon

Edited by Robert Klanten, Sven Ehmann,
Andrej Kupetz & Shonquis Moreno

gestalten

Table of Contents

004 Preface

012 From Our House Back to Bauhaus
016 *Saving the Planet in Style*
038 *From Rational Function to Romantic Function*
064 *From Recessionista to Pure Form Sublime*

086 Performing Arts and Crafts
090 *It's all about Context and Process*
096 *Processing Experience*
116 *Fluxus Furniture*
132 *Democratic Green*

136 A Tale Told by Design
140 *Folklore*
146 *Roustique References*
160 *Alchemy Experience*
178 *Luxury in Craft / Gracious Living*

202 Hunting and Collecting
206 *Juxtaposing*
214 *Archaic Nature*
232 *Shapeless — The New Ugly*
242 *Soft - Edged*
254 *Hard - Edged*
264 *Pixel Park*

266 Index

272 Imprint

from l. to r.: Arik Levy – *Fractal Light*, Christoffer Angell – *Lola Chair*,
Arik Levy – *Fractal Light*, Serhan Gurkan – *Fetish Gazelle*, Philippe Bestenheider – *Lui 6 Sofa*

from l. to r.: Elisa Strozyk – *Wooden Carpet*,
Tord Boontje – *Armoire*, Brodie Neill – *Pop*

from l. to r.: Asif Khan – *BBchair*,
Ronan and Erwan Bouroullec – *Clouds*

Bo Reudler – *Slow White Series*

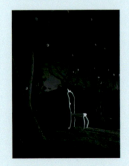

Design Beyond The Icon

There is increasing evidence to suggest that we are leaving behind the age of iconic design. _____

_____ It is not happening with particular haste, nor has this trend come totally out of the blue, nor did it catch us off guard with a purposeful vigour that might have made the global collapse of our economic system look slightly better. But it is happening nonetheless.

— *Andrej Kupetz* —

A shroud – woven from a mixture of new issues and fractured beliefs, doubts about ourselves and the system – is drawn over the icons and dulling their brilliance. Make no mistake, they still exist. They just no longer shine with the same intensity. There is a lingering suspicion that this period of transition towards a new epoch – this undefined no-man's land in which we find ourselves – appears so extreme precisely because we had previously made ourselves so comfortable in the age of iconic design. And because now – despite our enforced acceptance of the situation – we are essentially scared of what lies ahead.

It was without a doubt a wonderful time, one when it appeared so easy to obliterate the frontiers of existing thought in the design genre. Everything seemed possible. Even Andy Warhol's hypothesis of a future in which everyone would be famous for 15 minutes was given unimagined opportunities to be confirmed. The designer –

Mathias Hahn (2008)

as Ambra Medda, the icon of iconic design, once said – is the new pop star. And she was right. What went on in the field of design in recent years was the compositional equivalent of sex, drugs and rock'n'roll. The promise of a life as a pop artist – not hired out to industry but discovering one's market value in competition with fine artists, writers and musicians – seemed to be fulfilled over and over again. An entire generation was preoccupied with nothing less than catapulting the familiar and all-embracing genre of design into a whole new dimension of perception. They used techniques of exaggeration, hubris, theatricality and misleading information. In short, they used techniques of art.

Moustache (2009)

Design art – that new hybrid term – undermined the industrial values and notions of formal honesty that typified design concept during the first half of the 20th century. It also subverted the marketing-oriented design concept of the second half of the 20th century by making it look like a parody of itself. Design as a tool for distinguishing between different products was pushed to such extremes that the focus of attention was no longer on the product itself but on the design – and thus naturally on the designer as the generator of this interest. It was the designer alone who appeared capable of conquering and creating markets. Having outgrown the role of a service provider to industry, the designer strode confidently onto the stage of brand identity. Industry – partly aware of what was happening but also suffering in part from being immensely naive – assumed the role of a publisher, an impresario of design at the mercy of the designer's creative work (and, frequently enough, the designer). Because although a good number of industrial publishers could rightfully claim to have "made" their designers, many others were clearly out of their depth with the design work.

Design offered a new playground for the mechanisms of the art market: the creation of careers, the discovery and manufacturing of new stars – and all the accompanying unpleasant side effects. During this period, the cultural theory that wallpaper is the ugly sister of art was applicable to the entire discipline of design. The notion of iconic design placed little value on the concept of long-term quality and strove instead for the here and now. It pursued a kind of hysterical presence. It had to be seen and admired within a complex and confusing environment – and it had to possess that certain originality that made it recognisable. Iconic design had a creator and this creator had a recognisable style. Wherein lay the preordained limitations of iconic design? The number of styles available to their various protagonists for generating attention was insufficient in relation to the number of aspirants within the discipline. And what finally happened is what always happens when the public is in danger of losing touch. Systemisation and classification are the instruments for wresting the power of interpretation back from the creative and his chaos. And these are the instruments of the market – both in art and design art. With these tools at hand, the market set about dissecting iconic design. Suddenly the sketch of an aspiring hopeful was described as being *Bouroullecesque*, a futuristic lamp was *Newsonesque* and a chaise longue was *Hadidesque*. This

Nika Zupanc (2009)

form of classification degraded each work to the status of a copy, an imitation, just as wallpaper had once been the ugly sister of painting. In the end, the market was enraged by the mediocrity of the subsequent generations. And the same thing would have happened to us if an economic crisis of unprecedented enormity had not proved to be an even more effective weapon in challenging the justification for iconic design's enduring existence.

This is where we find ourselves today. In view of the worldwide economic crash, it is inevitable that auctions at which horrendous amounts of money are paid for prototypes and small series will appear out of touch with the times. But nothing more.

Iconic design has unquestionably added various facets to the definition of what the function of an object can be. An appliance can tell a story, be a work of art or a metaphor. And it can represent its owner in ways that had previously been reserved for cars and yachts. Furthermore, the individualisation and emotionalising of design was not merely part of the Zeitgeist. It was fun and – even more remarkably – it made absolute sense. In a world where everything occurs simultaneously and is highly visible, it is not as if styles such as iconic design simply disappear overnight. Styles no longer work as they did in previous eras. There is no giant pendulum constantly dictating time and direction to everyone and everything, no crystal ball that knows the absolute truth. Instead there are dozens of compass needles all constantly trying to re-orientate themselves. And in the rare event that most of them are pointing in the same direction for a brief instant, there will always be others pointing in the opposite direction. Even if the dominance of a particular style is broken, it still exists – weaker, certainly, but nevertheless still there in the background hum. Styles like these normally survive for a very long time, although their visibility and impact is severely reduced.

But for all that, now that the word "icon" seems to be approaching its expiry date, it is perhaps possible to breathe new life into the concept of design in the form of a new descriptive clarity. It is no coincidence that social questions have shaped many contemporary works of young designers and their mentors. While these are still isolated cases, they are put forward with genuine vehemence. It might be premature to speak of a turning point, but something widespread is definitely germinating. As Philipp Starck was recently heard saying in an interview, design lacks idealism and ethics. And if it wants to rediscover these values, it has to move into the core of the fundamental issues concerning the future of our society.

Today we can naturally only guess at the extent to which global economic crises, limited resources, environmental devastation and the growing world population will change lives around the planet in future. The only thing we know for certain is that these parameters will fundamentally transform our current lifestyles and usher in a new product and consumer culture. The question of the sustainability of all our actions – as creators, producers and consumers – is the first question we will always need to answer. It lies at the heart of deep future issues that design will have to tackle if it genuinely wants to regains its idealism.

There is a real danger that in the process of appropriating the term "sustainability", it becomes nothing more than the terminological heir of iconic design. Nevertheless, it is still worth attempting to use it as the starting point for a new ethics in design. Because a serious examination of the sustainability concept – away from all the short-term media hysteria that has surrounded it ever since Californian consumers woke up to their own ecological conscience – would be a marvellous opportunity to infuse designers and their work with revitalised social relevance.

Konstantin Grcic (2009)

But how can our world be organised in a sustainable manner? The role of design in this process needs to be evaluated with a rigorously critical eye. Beyond the attention-grabbing aspect and the flirtation with the art of the design avant-garde, the overwhelming mass of the design discipline is still too heavily embedded in the waning industrial age. As a consequence of increasingly saturated markets, it orients itself towards a sales policy within industry that is primarily focused on product differentiation for the purpose of tapping new markets. Yet product differentiation

on its own does not solve the pressing challenges of a sustainable lifestyle. The apparent product benefits – in the truest sense of the word – continue to be purely superficial.

Sustainable design, on the other hand, must take an entirely holistic approach and needs to consider the interrelationships within which design occurs. In this sense, it is contextual design and therefore the reincarnation of iconic design. Contextual design expands the concept of an object's function to include the period before its actual usage: by considering the raw materials used, the quality of social responsibility in production, and the carbon balance in production and logistics. Contextual design requires an object to be designed for technical and aesthetic durability, while possessing a high degree of compatibility with other products, and functionality in ways that neutralise social differentiation. Having reached the end of its useful life, the designed product or at least the materials used must be recyclable or at least disposable without causing harm.

Innovation is the driving force behind products that are manufactured, traded and disposed of under socially and environmentally fair conditions. If all of these factors are taken into consideration, it would be possible for a new ethical standard to emerge which could then evolve to form the basis of a sustainable design approach. It is not impossible. The discipline of

Raw-Edges (2009)

design has always grounded its self-image on a belief in its ability to change the world for the better – in the sense of a dynamic search to improve the quality of people's lives. This is an elitist belief which is often far removed from reality – particularly during times that are ruled by short-term marketing ideas. And yet in the face of the social and ecological revolutions now underway which have already developed into a civ-

Mario Botta (2009)

ilization-threatening scenario, it seems all the more important to reflect back on the roots of the discipline and its goal of shaping the world, to reinterpret that goal and to mobilise this attitude in approaching the tasks of the future. Designing our living environment in a sustainable way so that its quality is preserved – or thinking as we must in global terms, to ensure that the living environment actually has quality in the first place – is without doubt the major task facing design this century.

Sustainability could become the new guiding principle of design, the new ethical foundation of our creative efforts. The following seven theses are intended to help in shaping a home for the sustainable design concept. We realise that we are just at the beginning. But as pioneers searching for a greater quality of life on our planet, we are convinced that our level of knowledge will increase and that over the course of time we will be capable of refining the architecture of our home to perfection.

Sustainable design is ethical.

The first thesis touches on the attitude with which designers go about their daily business. The point here is to think in holistic terms. Questions about product benefit, social compatibility, lifespan, production, distribution, consumption and disposal must be posited at the beginning of each design task and we should be prepared to assume responsibility for the answers later on. Deciding not to design something – in other words, doing nothing – as a result of these deliberations can become part of the designer's new self-perception.

Sustainable design is complex.

This is not about understanding that green is the new white, but that answers to the reality of our times need to be found. Our world is digital. Back to nature and back to simplicity no longer work as principles because today's context is entirely different. So design will have to focus more on managing the complexity of our world and – given the advancing level of available technology – on channelling the user's desires and expectations so that a product, the result of a design process, will make a real contribution to raising the quality of that person's life.

Sustainable design impacts our environment as little as possible.

The underlying principle of our work is the realisation that every product created by man causes damage to the environment. So whenever we design anything, our highest priority must be to minimise the negative impact as far as possible. The consumption of materials and energy, the emission of harmful substances in production, the product's life cycle and its disposal all need to be taken into consideration, as does the product's social context, its ease of repair and the benefit to consumers of using a product over a long period of time.

Sustainable design is innovative.

In Western cultures, we seem to assume that innovation only takes place in conjunction with advanced technology and that it always produces an unprecedented product or a brand new service. We have to bid farewell to this notion if we genuinely want to arrive at a sustainable design approach. To design something means to conduct research into better products. But technological innovation is not always the central issue here. Only by pursuing rigorous and dynamic evolution across all product areas can we ever hope to obtain ultimately sustainable solutions. For example, new materials with novel properties can achieve sustainable effects in products of low complexity too. This type of thinking is essential in the long-term quest to decentralise and localise the production of everyday objects.

Sustainable design is aesthetic.

This thesis initially appears out of touch with the current climate, given the cultural diversity of the globalised world that is presently reflected in a diversity of styles, and given the extensive democratisation of general aesthetic sensibilities. Obviously we all have different ideas about what constitutes beauty. But still we perceive a harmony of proportions, materials, craftsmanship and details as being in some way aesthetic.

And we are not alone in holding a belief that is presumably determined by genetics. We recognise quality in an object. The greater an object's quality, the more aesthetic it becomes and the greater our willingness to use it for a long period. An object that is aesthetic in this sense is sustainable.

Richard Hutten (2008)

Sustainable design is authentic.

An authentic product demonstrates a high degree of social integrity. It represents an immediate and directly accessible benefit and therefore stands for value and identity. It possesses the ability to touch its user on an emotional level. In his 10 commandments of good design, the German designer Dieter Rams once expressed the sentiment as follows: "It doesn't try to make a product appear different – more innovative, more power-

ful, more valuable – than it actually is. It doesn't manipulate buyers and users, it doesn't incite them to self-deception." Even from today's perspective, nothing else needs to be added.

Sustainable design remains compatible with the future.

The last thesis on sustainable design offered at this juncture concerns the question about how far we can use our level of knowledge to influence the service life of a product. It looks at the future readiness of products and our ability to speculate in the right direction. Every product is part of a system, even if it appears to stand in isolation. It exists within the context of changing technology and the ensuing patterns of use. This is why the most sustainable products are the ones that retain their value and their usability over a long period of time. Choice of materials, production quality, aesthetic appeal, repair friendliness, construction and modular design can all be starting points for preserving the usefulness of the product as a whole, even if the incessant march of technology renders some part of the product obsolete.

Shigeru Ban (2009)

These ideas must be regarded as incomplete. Inevitably, they only describe our current state of knowledge about the possibilities for changing our product culture in sustainable ways. Initial examples of how this approach can be translated into concrete design are to be seen everywhere. If we can condense these so that the concept of sustainability gives rise to a worldwide movement in which design acquires a new and socially-motivated understanding of itself, the result would not be affordable luxury – it would be of essential importance to the survival of the entire discipline.

RICHARD HUTTEN

2008
Cloud chair
Material: Aluminium, nikkel platted
Photography: Ormond Editions
Producer: Ormond Editions

The chair is part of the research and the theme of basic forms which Richard Hutten has been working on his whole career. Specially the circle and the sphere shape have his interest in recent years.

From our house back to Bauhaus

Ninety years after its inception, Bauhaus now seems to be more alive than ever. _____

_____ The reason has less to do with the marketing activities that its inheritors – institutions and producers – dreamed up for its anniversary, and more to do with the enduring appeal of an ethical design approach which the school's protagonists originally devised.

Presumably the idea that a form can have an ethical dimension continues to strike most people as suspicious. But ever since Bauhaus, nothing has been designed without an active or at least passive examination of the product as a multilayered system. For any designer schooled in Bauhaus ideas – and thus for all designers who engage with classic modernism – every object has both a material level that refers to its concrete usage, and an immaterial level that tells us something about the attitude of the designer and which – according to current design theory – can be divided into aesthetic and symbolic functions. Not only do both levels have meaning for the creator, they also impact the behaviour of the user as an individual and part of society. Once infected with this mindset, neither of an object's two levels can be designed without regard for ethical considerations.

But why are we experiencing something of a Bauhaus renaissance at the precise moment of the school's anniversary? While the different levels of an object's design were regarded as being equally valuable at the time of Bauhaus – which was also a new industrial dawn when the needs of the masses were defined as vitally important – there has been a shift of emphasis in more recent times – times of saturated markets and superabundance, digitalisation and the rise of technology in almost all areas of life – to the immaterial level of design. And herein lies the presumably unavoidable danger of an absolute dominance of this level over the material one, thereby actually emptying the design process of its functional dimension. Both levels depend on one another – not least for explaining the design discipline and distinguishing it from art. Indeed, design's intense flirtation with art over the last few years must inevitably be followed by a period of sobering-up.

Here too, Bauhaus offers salvation in both form and meaning. Bauhaus and the subsequent epoch of International Style formulated a goal that involved nothing less than the education of society in the industrial age – with a type of design

that modelled itself on a stark lack of adornment of simple physical experimental procedures. Walter Gropius, the founder of the school, welded together design and ethics into a framework of social responsibility for the designer. And in the guidelines for Bauhaus production, he made vehement

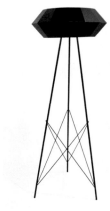

Jarrod Lim (2009)

demands for its implementation. The "multiplication of simplicity" and the "economical use of space, materials, time and money" would primarily serve to improve the quality of people's lives. The sober and rational design of Bauhaus products from 1925 onwards – to which critics quickly ascribed a "bicycle aesthetic" – conformed with Gropius's thinking on the efficient use of resources. If production costs could be reduced by saving on materials and using designs that were appropriate to the manufacturing process, products could be sold at lower prices. Broad sections of the population would then benefit because more affordable pricing would enable them to purchase the objects. Meanwhile, this type of design provided an irrevocable answer to the question of the designer's social commitment. The aesthetic that he/she assigned to the product's immaterial level foresaw the product benefit of making the world a better place.

There are two reasons why this approach failed to work in reality. Firstly, the aesthetic preferences of the target group were a long way removed from the revolutionary simplicity of Bauhaus's formal language. And secondly, the industrial production of furniture and utility items proved to be much too complicated and expensive to fulfil the promise of resource efficiency.

Saving the planet in style

And today? Is it once again the social question that has galvanised the design avant-garde to pursue creative ideas in the Bauhaus mode? In-

Arik Levy (2009)

evitably, this aspect is not at the foreground of the current Bauhaus renaissance. The return to the ethical dimension of design's immaterial level is determined more by ecological questions. The social question has not disappeared, but considering the parallel of poverty and wealth, early capitalism, communism and post-capitalism that we are now experiencing in globalised society, the global threat of climate change on its own seems to present a challenge that affects everyone in equal measure. In this sense, a shifting of attention to ecological issues has a deeply social meaning and is thus a logical continuation of Bauhaus ideas for the very reason that it has to answer questions of production, materials and suitability of form, as well as the problem of product benefit in terms of raising general quality of life. But for the designer, it is first and foremost a question of attitude: the seriousness of the situation places him/her in the exact position in which he/she feels most comfortable. His/her work is capable of saving the world – even though, or perhaps precisely because, it looks so good.

From rational function to romantic function

But what exactly does a design style look like if it draws its inspiration in the here and now from a movement that began over ninety years ago? Are the heirs of the "white gods" – in the words of the American author Tom Wolfe in his scathing Bauhaus critique *From Bauhaus to Our House* – still producing nothing other than "steel and glass boxes"? Wolfe's criticism was ostensibly aimed at Bauhaus but it was simultaneously a settling of scores with the whole of modernism. It is possible, for example, to view Le Corbusier's utopian housing units as prototypes of the modern housing silos that symbolise the dehumanisation of the residential environment and the failure of industrial solutions in architecture and design. It is the failure of a utopia. And it was – at least in practical terms – a mistake to define the concept of function as being a purely technical functioning that can be effortlessly duplicated and applied to all situations in life. The salient achievement of postmodernism and postmodern society is to have subjected the notion of function to a revision. Today we know that an object can fulfil numerous functions and that sometimes the emotional function (level) is far more important than the tangible one. And ever since a large part of our product world has been controlled by microchips which bundle an array of different functions into a single product, we also know that the external appearance of an object will never again be determined by a single unequivocal function. The guiding principle of classic modernism – form follows function – now only applies if the function is specifically defined in relation to a particular context.

When designers today refer to classic modernism in their work, it may well be for reasons of compositional simplicity, but it is inevitably executed with a postmodern attitude. While the concept of function in classic modernism was primarily assigned to a product's material level – i.e. the tangible product benefit – postmodern designers and users of their design are much more interested in assigning function to the product's immaterial level. To illustrate the point with a simple example: if a designer opts to use wood instead of plas-

Misewell (2008)

tic for a chair, the decision is not about using a cheap material that might, for example, prevent the user from sweating in summer. No, the designer opts for wood because this material better expresses his/her creative vision, or because wood creates a good ecological impression, or quite simply because the warmth of the material makes the chair seem more valuable. With these considerations, the designer is working on the immaterial level and clearly identifying it as the site where function is located. If the user or consumer is then faced with the choice of buying a chair that is plastic or wooden, he/she will reach a decision along the same lines because he/she already owns at least one chair to sit on. His/her needs are not defined by the material level of a product but are based on immaterial ideas that he/she wishes to fulfil.

Similar criteria apply to the concept of effectiveness which the Bauhaus founders demanded so vehemently of production. Except that today, the problem of finding a form that can be produced as rationally as possible is obsolete. Indeed, many of the products designed by the Bauhaus artists – such as Marianne Brandt's silverware – could not be industrially produced until the 1990s when technological standards of production finally reached a level that allowed the apparently simple but technically highly complex forms of the 1920s to be manufactured industrially. The Barcelona chair by Mies van der Rohe – so it was said jokingly but with an element of truth – took one day to build and another three to stop wobbling. But because digital production methods now make it possible to manufacture individual one-off everyday objects at prices comparable with mass-produced items, the cost aspect of rational design is almost entirely superfluous. And given that production in Western countries now only takes place wherever products can be differentiated from one another at the highest technological and qualitative level, the extent of a form's complexity is bound to incorporate a social component – the more complex a design becomes, the greater its probability of safeguarding jobs.

If in spite of this we are now seeing a large number of forms that appear rational or functional, having elevated formal simplicity to the height of a design principle, we are looking at design ideas that are dominated by the purely immaterial. What exudes from these wooden cabinets and enamelled hemispheres is unadulterated romanticism. That alone is their function.

From recessionista to pure form sublime

The stark transition from a synthetic product world to a seemingly authentic one adheres to the logic of social processes. An economic crisis on the scale that we are currently experiencing calls everything into question – the system and, because we live in postmodernism, its concrete manifestation. Anything that appears even slightly fake or superficial looks plainly obnoxious in the face of a crisis that is bringing a total rearrangement. Calls for genuine values, modesty and a sense of proportion are becoming louder. Meditation and inner purification are the principles of the moment. The same applies to the design of our environment. Iconoclasm of the kind demanded by Calvinist elements in the Reformation is the first step. The idols of the past are destroyed.

Simplicity in its most radical form rules the day. Nothing – not even something as structurally essential as a chair leg – can escape the suspicion of undue excess. Recessionista is a revolutionary style, one that has a particularly meticulous approach to the choice of materials and the politically opportune. But as everyone knows, the revolution devours its own children and things continue as before in greater moderation. People gradually become comfortable with the new simplicity of authenticity – with a certain serenity. What is currently emerging is not the somewhat cool minimalism of the 1990s but rather simplicity with a human face. The forms appear perfectly designed for the present moment, although their lightweight construction also lends them something transient and flexible. They are pure and yet sublime – presumably because they strike us as so useful. There is a seriousness in their choice of colour and material. Sealed grey surfaces harmonise with light untreated woods. These forms do not consider themselves to be more important than they are. They serve – and this is a goal we have not witnessed in design for a long time – the activities of work, reflection and contemplation. In short: all those things that strike us as so important in a time of crisis.

1

LIFEGOODS

2009
1 **At-At Walker Lamp**
   Material: Walnut veneer
   Photography: Tonatiuh Ambrosetti
   Producer: Ormond Contemporary Edition

A gangly floor lamp inspired by the ambulatory fighting machines from 'Star Wars: The Empire Strikes Back.'

TOMÁS ALONSO

2008
2 **Mr. Lights series**
   Material: Powder-coated steel, ash, T8 bulbs
   Photography: Luke Hayes,
   www.fluxstudio.co.uk

Alonso designed a series of lights around the new LED T8 tube light bulbs which, aside from being more energy-efficient and durable than standard fluorescent bulbs, also allows for more flexibility in the design by reducing the number of components and rendering a reflector shade unnecessary. Alonso's lights explore the formal continuity between the bulb and the fixture while playing with his materials.

2

1

NACHACHT

2009
1 Sideboard

2007 / 08
2 Hutfaenger Coat Rack

2009
3 Tipptisch Table and Chair
Material: Beech plywood, powder-coated
metal components
Photography: Jens Schwengel
Producer: nachacht

2

3

Saving the Planet in Style

BIG-GAME
Elric Petit, Augustin Scott de Martinville & Grégoire Jeanmonod

2008
1 Metal Work Lamp
  Material: Powder-coated aluminium profile
  Photography: ECAL / Florian Joye

2007
2 Wood Work Lamp
  Material: Balsa wood
  Photography: Fabrice Gousset
  Producer: Galerie kreo

The frame of *Wood Work lamp* is assembled from large balsa beams, a wood that is tyically used to make small-scale models. Producing a very limited edition object this way is appealing, the designers say, resulting in a monumental scale that is nonetheless accompanied by feather lightness (weighing in at 3.5 kg). The balsa is hardened with resin using the same technique employed in the fabrication of surfboards in their halcyon days.

MATHIAS HAHN

2008
3 Odd Cabinet
  Material: Ash, powder-coated Steel
  Photography: Lutz Sternstein
  Producer: Mathias Hahn

"It is an open secret that cupboards are often misused as just somewhere to stow things away – spontaneously and untidily," says the designer. Odd's powder-coated sheet-steel doors allow glimpses into the interior (order or disorder) of the cupboard and, hung on simple hinges made from wooden dowel, enhance the cupboard's two-dimensional appearance.

DANIEL ENOKSSON

2008
4 Pieces Stools and Bench
  Material: Pine, mdf & steel
  Photography: Måns Berg
  Producer: NC Möbler

1

FORMFJORD

2009
1 **Schweinchen Stackable Stools** (with storage)
Material: Coated OSB panels
Photography:Formfjord
Producer: Formfjord

FORM US WITH LOVE

2009
2 **Piccolo Side Table**
Material: Steel, board
Produced by Mitab

FREDRIK MATTSON

2009
3 **Moloss Lounge Chair**
Material: Solid wood, polyurethane foam
Producer: Vivero

2

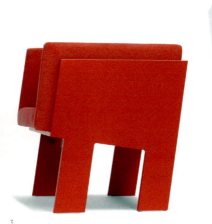

3

Saving the Planet in Style

1

2

3

4

MISEWELL
Vincent and Paul Georgeson

2008
1 Lockwood Chair
   Material: Steel, solid wood
   Producer: Misewell

2009
2 Lockwood Chair
   Material: Steel, walnut or maple
   Photography: Rat Race Studios
   Producer: Misewell

2008
3 Conrad Cafe Table
4 Conrad Cafe Table
   Material: Stamped steel, MDF, solid walnut
   Photography: Misewell
   Producer: Misewell

DENNIS NINO CLASEN

2009
5 Oscar X Lounger (prototype)
   Material: FSC-certified birch multiplex

OUT OF STOCK

2009
6 Naked Chair
   Material: Solid beech, powder-coated sheet steel
   Photography: OutofStock
   Producer: OutofStock

A furniture system that combines high-tech with tradition. A CNC 5 axis router cuts the chair's components into exact puzzle pieces with precise dovetails that allow the chair to be assembled and plugged into its stable position within minutes, without the need for any additional fixtures or tools. It can be taken down easily and reassembled numerous times, thus the design creates temporary seating à la folding chair. All parts can be stored flat without taking up much space or can find a more permanent use. The chair is the first in a range of a family of products based on this concept that will comprise a dining table, sidetable, stool and a bench.

5

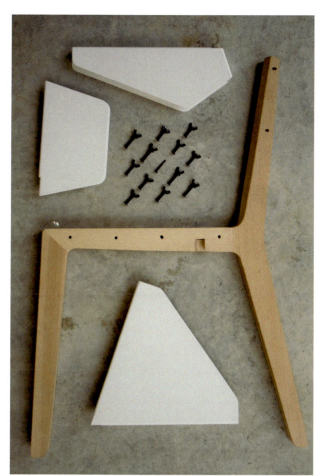

6

A chair that shows off its beautiful bones, allowing its skeleton to become its face. The designers undressed this seat but didn't leave it vulnerable: the construction allows folded steel sheets and beech wood to press against each other to become even stronger when sat upon. A CNC five-axis router cuts the chair's components into precise puzzle pieces that dovetail, allowing for easy assembly and creating a stable frame without the need for additional fixtures or tools. *Naked* packs flat for shipping and storage, and is the first in a family of products that will include a dining table, side table, stool and bench.

1

PELIDESIGN
Alexander Pelikan

2008
1 The PlasticNature Table and Chairs
Material: American walnut, ivory-coloured
polyurethene casting resin
Photography: Martin Stoop
Producer: PeLiDesign

2008
2 The PlasticNature Chair
Material: Oregon pine, coloured
polyurethene casting resin
Photography: Michael Anhalt
Producer: PeLiDesign

Both physically and stylistically, *The Plastic-
Nature series* underscores a connection between the organic and synthetic, the wooden
and the plastic. In the form of stools, chairs
and tables. In them, Pelikan has gracefully
fused crafted vernacular and injection-
molded furniture. He designed the shape
of the plastic connection in 3D software
and then rapid-prototyped the molds. During hand-casting, liquid resin flows into and
hardens in cavities milled into the wooden
seat and legs to form a dovetail connection.

2

PELIDESIGN
Alexander Pelikan

2007
1 **ClicDiner Chair**
2 **ClicLounger, ClicLounge Table**
Material: Bamboo five-layer plate 21 mm
Photography: Pirette van Poppel
Producer: PeLiDesign

2008
3 **ClicLounger Glass Miami**
Material: Pilkington hardened extra-clear
glass, European cherry wood
Photography: Neerle Amrein
Producer: PeLiDesign

With *ClicFurniture*, Pelikan sought to translate the ideas of the Modernists into the digital age. The connection of wood and glass became possible only through close collaboration with expert craftsmen and by pushing the limits of advanced production techniques like CNC diamond milling. For the designer, Clic demonstrates the power of what he calls "digital craftsmanship."

1

2

TAKESHI MIYAKAWA DESIGN

2009
1 **Stump Chair**
Material: Torched fir plywood
Photography: Takeshi Miyakawa

SEBASTIAN ERRAZURIZ

2008
2 **Repisa N5**
Material: Wood

1

3

2

DUEESTUDIO
Claudia & Harry Washington

2009
1 Kana Chair
Material: Wood
Photography: Milvio Attili
Producer: DUEestudio

2009
2 Cavado Table
Material: Wood
Photography: Harry Washington

FOR USE
For Use / Numen

2009
3 YY chair
Material: Varnished solid oak wood,
plywood, foam, fabric
Photography: For Use
Producer: Moroso

REINHARD DIENES

2009
4 3,60 Degree II Table Lamp
Material: Steel, tinted glass and textile
Photography: Reinhard Dienes

2009
5 La Grand Floor Lamp
Material: Walnut wood, steel and textile
Photography: Reinhard Dienes

4

5

Saving the Planet in Style

1

CASIMIRMEUBELEN
Casimir

2009
1 Zak n2 Shelving
2 Zak n1 Shelving
   Material: Solid oak and leather
   Photography by Kristof Vrancken
   Produced by CasimirMeubelen

Again looking to everyday objects for inspiration, Casimir builds on the concept of an ordinary plastic shoulder or messenger bag to create shelving and cabinets.
260 x 43 x 61 cm.

LAB::ISTANBUL
lab::istanbul

2009
3 Merduban Shelving
   Material: Wooden ladder
   and lacquered shelves
   Photography by Bediha Gungor

Merduban gives new purpose to mass-produced objects, lending users a new perspective on ubiquitous objects. In this case, lab::Istanbul have transformed a wooden ladder into a bookcase that can stand alone or be added to modularly.

2

3

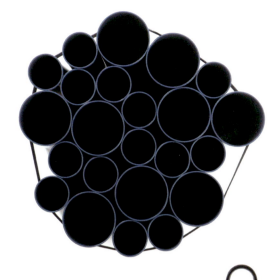

PIERO LISSONI
Piero Lissoni for Porro

2006
1 Camogli Chair
Material: Oak or "carbone" oak, woven straw
Producer: Porro
Photography: Tommaso Sartori

LORIS ET LIVIA
Loris Jaccard, Livia Lauberl

2008
2 Umbrella Stand (prototype)
Material: Powdercoated aluminium, pvc lids, nylon
Photography: James Champion

2009
3 Screen and Side Chair
Material: Solid oak, textile, nylon
Photography: James Champion

French designers Jaccard and Lauberl cleverly combine partition and storage.

1

2   3

MOTOKI YOSHIO

2008
1 **T 01 Cabinet**
2 **Z 01 Cabinet**
3 **E 02 Cabinet**
4 **E 01 Cabinet**
   Material: Paulownia wood
   Photography by Takumi Ota
   Produced by Paulownia

Paulownia is a type of wood that has been used in making traditional Japanese chests and other furniture for more than 200 years. Paulownia has the virtues of being lightweight, limber and impervious to humidity, fire and pests. In Japan, these qualities made Paulownia highly coveted in the storage of kimonos and other valuable property. Today the traditional forms made from Paulownia are being updated by modern designers like Yoshio while maintaining superior craftsmanship.

4

NAOKI HIRAKOSO

2008
1 **H 05 Bench**
 Material: Wood (Paulownia)
 Produced by Paulownia
 Bench

All of Hirakoso's pieces, like this bench, are hand-made by the craftsmen of the Kamo Chest Manufacturer's Cooperative in Niigata prefecture.

2

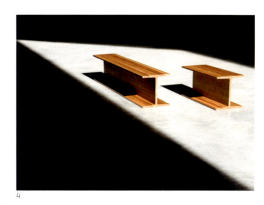

4

CASIMIRMEUBELEN
Casimir

2008
2 **Kist n2 Cabinet**
3 **Kist n1 Cabinet**
 Material: Solid oak
 Photography by Kristof Vrancken
 Produced by CasimirMeubelen

Taking his cue from the industrial forms of such workaday objects as the crate, Casimir turned a wooden box for transporting furniture into a piece of furniture itself.
Kist n°2. 180 x 50 x 120 cm
Kist n°1. 80 x 120 x 60 cm

2008
4 **Poutrel Bench**
 Material: Solid Oak
 Photography by Annick Geenen
 Produced by CasimirMeubelen

With Poutrel, Casimir transformed the universally familiar form of the construction industry's I-beam into a bench or table base.

3

2007
1 Curiosity Cabinet
Material: Wood

Icelandic Studio Bility offers a metaphor, the interpretation of a personality and a labyrinthine storage or display cabinet, all in one object.

MARINA BAUTIER

2008
2 Fold Chair
Material: Solid oak, wool, polyurethane foam, powder-coated steel

Consuming little space when folded away, fold nonetheless maintains the comfort of a generously proportioned lounge chair.

1

2

1

2

3

KASPAR HAMACHER

2008
1 Das Brett / The Board Shelf
Material: Massiv wood
Photography: A. Condes
Producer: Kaspar Hamacher

Because the upper surface of this shelf is concave, the books lean against each other for support. The uncurved underbelly of the shelf, however, provides a subtle visual counterpoint.

2009
2 Der Lederriemen / The Leather Belt Shelf
Material: Leather, stainless steal
Photography: A. Condes

A cow-leather belt combined with gravity generates a storage space for books. Through its shape and materiality, this product becomes suggestive of elemental organic forces while preserving its fundamental clarity.

MARINA BAUTIER

2009
3 Lap Shelving
Material: Oak, powder-coated metal
Producer: Caser

Lap shelving is a modular storage system that combines low production costs with high-quality aesthetics and function. Laser-cut, creased and powder-coated metal shelves and storage units are integrated into a simple oak frame, creating consoles and bookshelves alike.

1

KRÄUTLI
Florian Kräutli

2008
1 Stacking Nesting Tables
Material: Cardboard
Photography: Florian Kräutli

An expandable nesting table that shelters smaller tables, which can serve as additional surfaces, trays, drawers or stands, or stack vertically to form a higher table and shelf unit.

CATE&NELSON DESIGN

2008
2 Crisis Shelving
Material: Base in solid wood
Photography: cate&nelson design
Produced: cate&nelson design

Crisis is a piece of furniture intended to keep users in mind of the times in which we are living – our values, our wishes, our worries. Observing that most people place ornaments (instead of essential items, items that are "necessary" to making a home more cosy and one's own) on their shelves, the designers integrated various permanent objects into the crisis shelf to stand as symbols of the Zeitgeist.

2

MAARTEN KOLK & GUUS KUSTERS

2008
1 Cultivation Cabinet
Material: Oak, cotton
Photography: Maarten Kolk

In Kolk and Kusters' work, nature emerges as an important theme, not merely as inspiration or decoration, but giving the object organic qualities that often suggest growth. Cultivation is a cupboard in which one can grow plants indoors. By placing the outside inside, the designers ask users to focus on a natural process.

2007
2 Solitary Table
Material: Oak, leather, walnut details
Producer: Lebesque

A classically familiar, and even archetypal object, the kitchen table, was the inspiration for *Solitary*. The designers found the conventional table too cumbersome and sought to create a more intimate space. This one-person table includes an extending leaf mechanism that, though typically hidden, is made visible here.

HUNDREDS TENS UNITS

2009
3 A-Series Storage Unit (prototype)
Material: Oak, birch plywood, Oriented Strand Board (OSB), Medium-Density Fibreboard (MDF), acrylic
Prototype by A&B Homecare

Inspired by ISO paper sizing, this storage unit was constructed from various grades of material, each more processed than the last. The units can be assembled individually or modularly.

Saving the Planet in Style

1

2

SEMIGOOD DESIGN
Thom Jones

2008
1 **Rian End Table**
2 **Rian Bench**
  Material: White ash
  Photography: Semigood Design
  Producer: Semigood Design
4 **Rian Bar Stool**
  Material: Walnut

DUEESTUDIO
Claudia & Harry Washington

2007
3 **Lola Chaise Longue**
  Material: Wood and cotton cord
  Photography: Harry Washington
  Producer: DUEestudio

BRIKOLÖR

2009
5 **Älta-Älta Stool**
  Material: Solid ash, varnished ash veneer
  or padded leather
  Photography: Niclas Löfgren
  Producer: Brikolör

Brikolör, run by three carpenters, an architect and one journalist, designs and manufactures furniture in Göteborg, Sweden "with a guaranteed emotional and technical durability of 300 years."

BUBBLEUPROJECT
Kyung Sunghyun and Jeon Geehee

2009
6 **BubbleuProject Table With Lamp** (prototype)
  Material: Wood, ceramic
  Photography: Kyung Sunghyun

Bubbleuproject prefer nature over nurture and one product over the wasteful purchase of two. For this office or home desk, they use a wood-ceramic combo instead of plastic while integrating a task lamp into a table.

3

4

5

OUT OF STOCK

2009
7 Arbor Compact Desk
Material: Oak, teak, maple, wenge
and sucupira (solid) woods
Photography: OutofStock
Producer: OutofStock

6

7

Stefan Diez brings order to the chaos he create. His *Ideal House* for the imm Cologne furniture fair featured rooms in several "buildings." Significantly, Diez's domestic space assumes multiple functions not usually associated with the home: public space, social space (in the form of a bar), a workshop. The bathroom, with its unpainted sheetrock walls, minimal storage, seating and accessories, suggests that life is a prolonged work in progress where the tools for living always remain within easy reach.

CH04 Houdini (2009)

After studying architecture and practicing carpentry, Diez travelled to India, where he designed and built furniture for a year. On returning to Germany in 1996, he resumed his studies at the State Academy of Art and Design in Stuttgart, this time in industrial design. While still a student, he worked for Richard Sapper in the U.S., and then Munich-based Konstantin Grcic. In 2003, Diez established his own Munich studio, designing products, furniture and exhibitions. Within only two years, Germany's *Elle* Decoration magazine selected him as newcomer of the year.

Diez has proven himself a modern classicist, of sorts, someone who creates products for real life that are not merely intended to appear stylish, but that work and last. He has a talent for creating objects and stripping them bare in ways that add great value. The multi-purpose *Big Bin* storage system for Authentics comprises ABS plastic containers that can be stacked vertically and horizontally, by interlocking handles located on their sides. His *Bent* seating for Moroso is aptly named: cut from sheets of steel, each colourful piece is bent along large-scale perforations. The child-like quality of the seams formed by the perforations is inversely proportionate to the sophistication of the geometric shapes they create. For Thomas, the designer created a line of stainless steel cookware called *Genio* that can be taken directly from stove to tabletop thanks to their simple porcelain shells, which also keep the food warm. Diez's aptly titled and puffy tufted *Couch* for Elmar Flötotto has a cellular structure that folds flat for inexpensive shipping. The sofa takes its final form only at its destination where it is filled with polystyrene balls. At times, Diez gives users solutions that are exceedingly straightforward: the larger proportions of his *Tema* flatware for Rosenthal-Thomas were a response to today's larger food portions. At other times, the solution only appears to be irreducibly simple.

The seating that Diez has produced for the likes of Thonet *(404)*, Wilkhahn *(Chassis)*, Promosedia *(Friday)* and E15 *(Houdini)* are likely to become familiar to the mainstream consumer through less articulate but widely circulated knock-offs – and this should only be taken as a compliment. Imitation remains the sincerest form of flattery.

www.stefan-diez.com

2009
CH04 Houdini
Material:Oak veneered plywood, laquered
Photography:IngmarKurth
Producer: E15

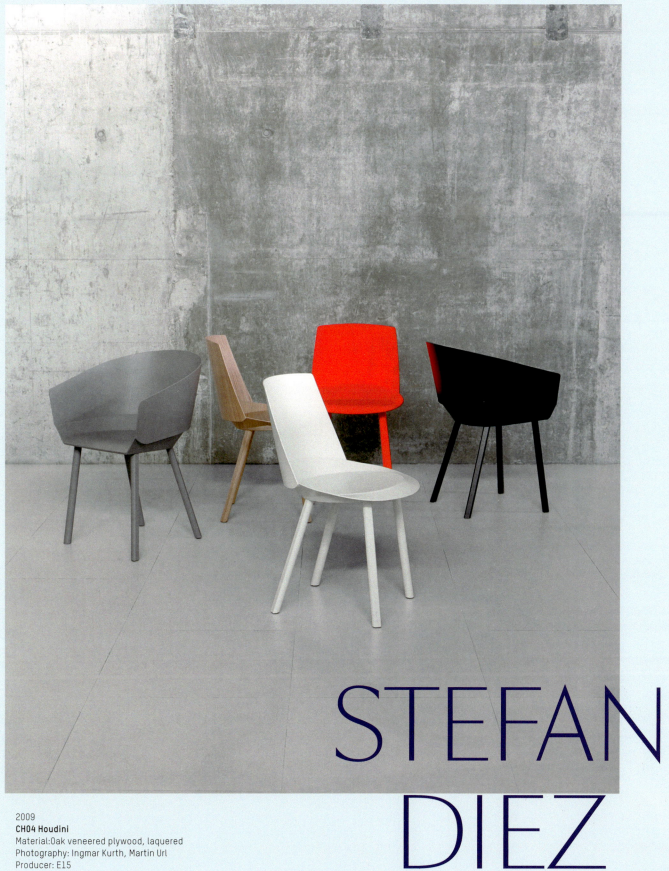

2009
CH04 Houdini
Material:Oak veneered plywood, laquered
Photography: Ingmar Kurth, Martin Url
Producer: E15

STEFAN DIEZ

Saving the Planet in Style

MOUSTACHE

François Azambourg, Big-Game, Matali Crasset,
Ana Mir, Emili Padros, Inga Sempé

2009
Début collection
Photography: Les arts Décoratifs, Paris / Tania et Vincent

Established by Stéphane Arriubergé and Massimiliano
Iorio (of Paris-based Domestic design shop), Moustache
represents the pair's effort to unite a group of like-minded
designers to create enduring and innovative furnishings.
The debut collection includes abstractly modern pieces that
already have the strength of classics

KENSAKU OSHIRO

2009
1 Soft Step Ladder
Material: Steel, polyurethane foam, fabric
Photography: Beppe Brancato

STUDIO DROR
Dror Benshetrit

2009
2 Peacock Chair
Material: Felt
Producer: Cappellini

LORIS ET LIVIA
Loris Jaccard & Livia Lauber

2009
3 Low Seat
Material: Wood, foam, textile
Photography: James Champion

2009
Kente Seat and Side Table
Material: Steel rod frame, varnished aluminium tube shell,
handwoven brown-black or multicolour tape
Photography: Varaschin
Producer: Varaschin

1

2

3

KILIAN SCHINDLER

2008
1 Light
Material: Coated steal, waterproofed wood
Producer: Kilian Schindler

IMAGINARY OFFICE
Daniel Hedner

2009
2 Minilamp
Material: Powder-coated aluminium, polished brass
Photography: Karl Sandoval

STUDIO GORM

2008
3 Cloud Lamp (prototype)
Material: Fabric, laminated polystyrene, fiberglass rod, beech wood
Photography: Studio Gorm
Producer: Studio Gorm

1

JARL FERNAEUS

2009
1 James Chair and Oak Out Table
Material: Oak, powder-coated aluminium
Photography: Magnus Cramer
Producer: Jarl Fernaeus Design

2009
2 Friendly Office Lamp
Material: Powder-coated metal and pine wood
3 Shell Lamp
Material: Ash wood
Photography: Magnus Cramer
Producer: Jarl Fernaeus Design

STUDIO GORM

2008
4 #3 Chair (prototype)
Material: Ash and oak plywood with lacquered
milk paint and Douglas fir plywood
Photography: Studio Gorm
Producer: Studio Gorm

2   3   4

MISO SOUP DESIGN
Daisuke Nagatomo & Minnie Jan

2008
K Workstation
Material: Plywood
Photography: Daisuke Nagatomo & Minnie Jan
Producer: MisoSoupDesign

K Workstation incorporates bamboo-laminated plywood to create highly efficient work surfaces. The ribbon-like shape provides both shelving and desk space in a single unit.

PUNGA AND SMITH

2009
1 Fruit Baskets
Material: American oak, stainless steel

Fruit Baskets is a concept for wall-mounted fruit storage and preservation that reminds users of picking fruit directly from a tree.

TAKESHI MIYAKAWA DESIGN

2009
2 Zero Shift Bench / Storage Unit
Material: Lacquered ultralight MDF
Photography: Takeshi Miyakawa

An oval bench sectioned diagonally and hiding storage in each half.

From Rational Function to Romantic Function

2008
1 **Bone Stool**
   Material: White Carrara marble or black Belgian marble, oak
2 **La Flèche Stool**
   Material: Corian® in «White Glacier», walnut
   Photography: YMER&MALTA
   Producer: YMER&MALTA

1

2

MISO SOUP DESIGN
Daisuke Nagatomo & Minnie Jan

2007
1 Za Stool
Material: Plywood
Photography: Daisuke Nagatomo & Minnie Jan

1

MATHIAS VAN DE WALLE

2009
2 L (Stackable) Chair
Material: Wood

A three-legged chair made from twin panels
of CNC-milled wood.

2

SHIGE HASEGAWA

2009
1 Hana Table
Material: Birch plywood

SANDER MULDER

2 Crow Trestle Table
Material: European oak, smoked glass

TOMITADESIGN
Kazuhiko Tomita

 2003
1 ELY Chair
    Material: Metal, felt
    Producer: COVO

MILE

 2008
3 Graft Armchair
    Material: Frame and seat in silicon rubber,
    legs in solid beech
    Photography: Takumi Ota Photography

GREIGE
Daniel Lorch

 2008
2 Kontisch Table
    Material: Steel, glass, concrete

2

3

From Rational Function to Romantic Function
49

Product designer Sebastian Herkner updates traditional crafts and exploits modern digital technologies, combining diverse materials and techniques in a way that generates a fresh aesthetic. Produced in a limited edition of 100, *Perserfell* is a hybrid object: a Persian carpet at first glance, but one actually cut in the familiar shape of an animal-skin rug.

While Herkner's maple wood and leather *Albion* chair recalls a bygone era (think stenographers and secretaries), it has proportions that make it new. With his Kate seat the designer thoroughly modernized the antique wing chair. To do so, he combined unexpected, contrasting materials and colours – a knitted textile, wool-covered shell, slim cushions and

nan16 (2009)

a robust metal brace with chunky wooden legs – and took advantage of a new 3D-knitting technology to fabricate the arcing back of the chair (to which he then attached the upholstered shell as one might belt a saddle to a horse). As the sitter reclines, the knit gives way until it comes to rest against the industrial metal brace with a reassuring solidity.

The designer collaged materials again in his 2009 *Bell light* and *Bell table*. The table has a mouth-blown, tinted glass base and a brass top that brings to mind both craft and industry, old and new. His (again, industrial-looking) *Bell light* – composed of maple wood, with changeable copper, steel and fabric shades – was inspired by spotlights and photographers' reflectors, and can be arranged in various directions to emphasize its light-focusing capacity. *Bell* generates a different light temperature and colour, and therefore mood, depending on the material of the shade used, and can be carried conveniently by rolling up the power cord and affixing it to a handle. Herkner went back to basics, on the other hand,

with *Bulb+*, a simple electric bulb fitted, via UV adhesive, with a glass loop. The integrated loop makes it possible for users to hang *Bulb+* to anything as rudimentary as a nail or hook and to get more sophisticated from there.

Born in 1981 in Bad Mergentheim, Germany, Herkner graduated in industrial design from the Academy of Art and Design in Offenbach am Main (where he now teaches) in 2007. He established his own studio earlier, however, in 2006. Today, Herkner's diverse clientele includes Chanel, a number of national banks, Material Connexion, the Messe Frankfurt Exhibition, and Stella McCartney Ltd. (for whom he interned in London before graduation). For Lufthansa he designed in-flight tableware. For the Frankfurt Botanical Garden, he created a spare but cosy market area with wood-and-metal benches and bins for the display of potted plants. This consistently clean reconciliation of opposites, including classic and forward-looking aesthetics, materials and concepts, makes Herkner's objects and installations both fresh and familiar.

www.sebastianherkner.com

2009
Nan16 Lighting
Material: Aluminium, leather, acrylic glass
Photography: Sebastian Herkner
Producer: nanoo

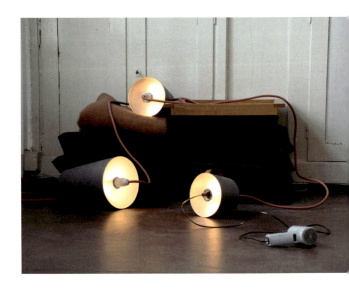

SEBASTIAN HERKNER

2009
1 **Bell-Table**
   Material: Tinted glass and brass
   Photography: Sebastian Herkner
   Producer: nanoo

2009
2 **Bell-Table, Bell-Light & Albion Chair**
   Material: Wood, paper, tabe
   Photography: Sebastian Herkner

From Rational Function to Romantic Function

ALISON BERGER GLASSWORKS

2009
1 **Mirrored Pendant Chandelier**
   Material: Crystal, oxidized coloured glass,
   brushed nickel hardware
   Photography: Jonathan Allen for Holly Hunt
   Producer: Alison Berger Glassworks

Inspired by mercury glass and the complex silhouettes of
Baroque chandeliers, Berger's chandelier features coloured
glass that is oxidized on the surface of each of the 25 crystal pendants, resulting in a reflective sterling silver effect,
which, when lit, glows red.

KRANEN/GILLE

2008
2 **Plant Side Table**
   Material: Nickel-plated steel, lacquered ash

3 **Plant Lamp**
   Material: Gilded steel, Pyrex glass, light fixture
   Photography: Frans Lossie
   Producer: Kranen/Gille

For the *Plant* series the designers envisioned an industrial
growth that grows to perform a certain function.

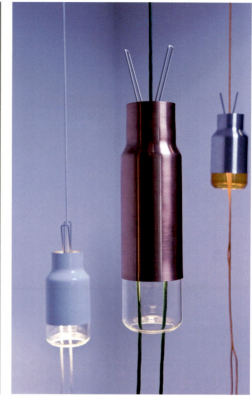

5

ARIK LEVY

2009
4 Russula.MGX Light
Material: Epoxy
Producer: .MGX by Materialise

The *Russula.MGX* light object takes its name and shape from a mushroom – one of nature's most fascinating creations; fast growing and delicate, with both architectural and structural qualities, it reveals the most beautiful intricacies when sliced.

MATHIAS HAHN

2008
5 Lantern
Material: Aluminium, copper, glass
Photography: Luke Hayes
Producer: Mathias Hahn

Wholly adjustable in terms of how low or high it hangs by means of a clamp mechanism situated inside the lamps that slides along its cord, *Lantern* locates itself typologically somewhere between a floor and pendant lamp.

DUNCAN BULL

2009
6 Kink Lamp
Material: Gold-plated steel frame
Producer: ErnestHoward

MARC VENOT

2004
7 Boule Light (prototype)
Material: PMMA, black-lacquered steel, water, PS ball
Photography: V. Huyghes

Venot's light alters with a mere movement of the hand.

6

7

From Rational Function to Romantic Function

53

1

2

FREDRIK FÄRG

2008
1 Something Rug-Stool-Basket

As a designer, Färg prefers to works with surprise and change. Something can be transformed from a rug into a stool, and then turned upside-down to form a basket or storage unit.

STOKKEAUSTAD

2009
2 Lobby Chair
Material: Steel, foam, upholstery
Photography: Casamania
Producer: Casamania

PHILIP MICHAEL WOLFSON

2008
3 BookCurve I
Material: Corian
Photography: Maxim Nilov
Other project credits: Jessica Altenburger, Richard Hartle
Producer: Solidity

2009
4 Why Console
Material: Corian
Photography: Maxim Nilov
Other project credits: Richard Hartle
Producer: Solidity

3

4

From Our House Back to Bauhaus

54

1

2

3

JONAS LYNDBY JENSEN DESIGN
Jonas Lyndby Jensen

2009
1 **Wooden Spoon Chair** (prototype)
Material: Soap-treated ash, horsehair textile designed and woven by Jacob Bille
Photography: Jonas Lyndby Jensen
Other credits: Textile is designed and made by Jacob Bille

Jonas Lyndby Jensen &
Morten la Cour

2007
5 **Twist Chair** (prototype)
Material: Cross-stiffened pipe construction, Hallingdal textile from Kvadrat
Photography: Jonas Lyndby Jensen and Morten la Cour

GÄRSNÄS

2 **Loop Coat Rack**
Material: Wood
Photography: Casamania
Producer: Casamania

AUTOBAN
Seyhan Özdemir& Sefer Çağlar

2008
3 **Nest Throne Chair**
Material: Oak, leather
Photography: Mustafa Nurdogdu
Producer: Autoban

FREDRIK FÄRG

2009
4 **RE:cover Chair Series**
Material: Salvaged chairs with a new 100% recyclable polyester felt upholstery
Producer: Fredrik Färg

Färg treated the chair like a fashion model, creating bespoke dresses for rescued seating.

4

5

Saving the Planet in Style

1

2

DITTE HAMMERSTROEM

2008
1 Leggy Cabinets
Material: Bog oak
Photography: Jeppe Gudmundsen-Holmgreen

2008
2 Haslev Remix Storage Unit
Material: Varnished oak, woollen yarn
Photography: Jeppe Gudmundsen-Holmgreen
Producer: Haslev Møbelsnedkeri

Storage furniture with a basket that is a reinterpretation of
the classic sewing tables from Haslev Møbelsnedkeri.

2002
1 **Chair for the Person Wishing to be Heard**
Material: Wood, steel
Photography: Jeppe Gudmundsen-Holmgreen

2007
2 **Small Tall Stools**
Material: Stained oak, plastic string
Photography: Jeppe Gudmundsen-Holmgreen

1

2

From Rational Function to Romantic Function

FREDRIK MATTSON

2009
1 **Koja Armchair**
2 **Koja Sofa**
Material: Polyether foam, wood, veneer, fabric
Producer: Bla Station

GÄRSNÄS

3 **Kvilt Sofa**
Material: Fabric

1

3

2

1

NIKA ZUPANC

2009
1 **Tapisserie and Phonique / Sofas in C Minor**
   Material: Lacquered wood, fabrics
   Photography: Dragan Arrigler
   Producer: La Femme et La Maison

CHRISTIAN VIVANCO

2009
2 **Our Little White Sofa**
   Material: Steel, cushions
   Photography: Christian Vivanco

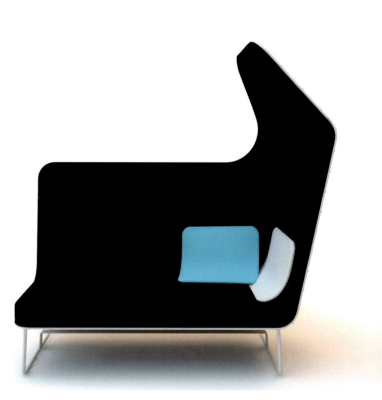

2

From Rational Function to Romantic Function

1

PATRICIA URQUIOLA

2009
1 Armchair and Sofa
Material: Wood, textile
Producer: Moroso

A sofa intended to stand in the middle of the room instead of against the wall, as is traditional in Uzbekistan where the designer found her inspiration for the collection. She combined traditional Uzbek weaving techniques with modern industrial manufacturing methods.

EDWARD VAN VLIET

2009
2 Sushi Seating
Material: Fabric
Producer: Moroso

For Moroso, Dutch designer van Vliet collages Japanese and Moroccan themes through upholstery and rounded cushions.

PHILIPPE BESTENHEIDER

2009
3 Binta Chairs
Material: Injected polyurethane foam, steel frame, removable fabric cover
Photography: Moroso
Producer: Moroso

Binta's sculptural shape evokes African wood carvings, but its polyurethane forms are softer. *Binta* roots itself to the ground with a thick trunk whose nonetheless elegant form brings to mind the weighty wizened baobab. Its upholstery is a patchwork of Wax fabrics, the traditional brilliant, clashing textiles worn by African women. *Binta* is also available in plain fabrics, but it would be a shame.

2

3

PATRICIA URQUIOLA

2009
1 **Rift Armchair**
   Material: Fabric
   Produced by Moroso

RYAN DART DESIGN

2008
2 **Jersey Bench**
   Material:Gel coat, walnut, aluminium
   Photography by ryandartdesign

1

PETTER SKOGSTAD

2009
1 Salone Satellite 2009 Exhibition
    Photography: Mads Hårstad Pålsrud

Skogstad imagined a Nordic lounge or living room to introduce his new furniture in Milan. He focused on the Scandinavian philosophy that embraces simplicity, longevity, quality, pragmatism, honesty and, where appropriate, environmentally aware design.

TOKUJIN YOSHIOKA

2008
2 Mermaid Chair
    Material: Polypropylene
    Producer: Driade

Yoshioka developed *Mermaid* from 2D to 3D, as if it were origami, using rotational molding, the same technique he used to produce his Tokyo-Pop Chair. The form was conceived by folding a simple round sheet by hand. "The challenge of this project," the designer says, "was to enhance and cultivate the form as if it was not deliberately designed, but born naturally."

2

From Rational Function to Romantic Function

2009
Monza Armchair
Material: Ash wood, polypropylene
Producer: Plank

KGID's stackable armchair bridges wood and plastic via injection moulding and hence imbues the artisanal roots of Plank with the characteristics of modern industrial design.

REINHARD DIENES

2009
1 **Juan Stool**
  Material: Polypropylene
2 **Pedro Stool**
  Material: Polypropylene (paper mockups)
  Photography: Reinhard Dienes

Dienes' stackable chairs *Juan*, *Pablo* and *Pedro* are made of flexible plastic and produced from a flat, milled component. Each surface is stretched and compressed to form a closed, stable system.

JANG WON YOON

2007
3 **Janus Chair** (prototype)
  Material: Polyurethane foam
  Photography: Jang Won Yoon

Yoon's glossy chairs are both foldable and stackable.

BOUROULLEC BROTHERS
Ronan and Erwan Bouroullec

2008
Vegetal Chair
Material: Dyed polyamide
Photography: Paul Tahon and Ronan Bouroullec
Producer: Vitra

Vegetation served as inspiration for this aptly named stacking indoor/outdoor chair. Its plant-like structure was made of polyamide and stretched production techniques to the limit. *Vegetal* is offered in six colours, unusual for plastic chairs, all of which emphasise the link to nature.

1 **Tension Magazine Rack** (concept)
   Material: Gas-injected polypropylene or Hyreck or die-cast
   aluminium
   Photography: Alain Gilles / The Studio

Gilles focused on the structure of this product, envisioning
it as a piece of macro (if not quantum) architecture. Using
plastic injection, Gilles intends to manufacture the product
by slotting together two similar pieces, reducing the cost of
the mould, stocking and shipping.

1

2

SAMARE
Laurie and Mania Bedikian, Nicolas Bellavance-
Lecompte, Patrick Meirim de Barros

2009
2 **MOUNTIE**
   Material: Steel frame, nylon webbing
3 **TESTAN**
   Material: Stee, rawhide
   Photography: SAMARE
   Producer: SAMARE

From the native (Canadian) Huronne word for "stop," *Testan*
is a handcrafted hexagonal table with a tensioned skin surface held together by an elegant triangular lacing woven into
its underbelly.

3

A.G. FRONZONI

1964/2009
1 '64 Tables, Chairs, Bench
Producer: Cappellini

SERHAN GURKAN

2008
2 Golden Ratio-Beautiful Units
Modular Bookcase
Material: Wooden panel, plexiglass boxes
Photography: Okan Guler
Producer: Serhan Gurkan

This is just a (colourful) box generated from the Golden Ratio, according to the Istanbul-based designer, yet no matter how many you combine and in which direction, they will always carry the elegance of their human proportions. "Every day you will be your own designer," Gurkan says.

1

2

WARM & STOLZENBURG
Corinna Warm

2008
1 Slice Side Tables
Material: Powder-coated steel
Photography: Klas Strom

JASPER MORRISON

2009
2 Bac Chair
Material: Wood
Produced by Cappellini

PATRICK NORGUET

2009
3 Steel Chair and Stool
Material: Steel
Producer: Lapalma

Tokyo-based Shigeru Ban has given new meaning to the phrase "paper architect." Five months following the catastrophic Kobe earthquake in January 1995, when locals were still reduced to living in tents, Ban responded by designing an inexpensive paper-based shelter that could be built by literally anyone. Each 16-square-meter structure perched atop a "foundation" of sand-filled yellow Kirin beer crates with paper tubes for walls and canvas ceilings and roofs. The tubes, readily available in a variety of thicknesses and diameters, were easy to transport, store, assemble on-site and recycle after use. During the Kobe crisis, Ban was also constructive in less literal ways: he established a non-governmental organization called the Voluntary Architects Network and became a consultant to the United Nations High Commissioner for Refugees. A paper church he built for the recovering city remains standing today.

10-Unit System (2009)

Born in Tokyo in 1957, Ban studied architecture at the Southern California Institute of Architecture and the Cooper Union School of Architecture in New York, and then worked for Arata Isozaki in Tokyo before founding his own local practice in 1985. Coming from the deeply sophisticated craft-based culture of Japan, with its much-venerated handmade paper called *washi*, it seems natural that Ban began to explore the structural use of paper at different scales in 1985. The architect began to pioneer the architectural use of paper tube structures in earnest in 1989 with the *Paper Arbor* in Nagoya. After six months, assaulted by wind and rain, the hardening of the glue and exposure to UV rays actually fortified the tubes instead of compromising them. For Ban, however, sustainability is a fundamental element of design, and he has little patience discussing it as a trend. His genius has been to – poetically – exploit card-

board's capacity, though recycled, to be moulded into load-bearing columns, waterproofed and made fire-resistant, bent into trusses and rapidly assembled by applying self-adhesive waterproof sponge tape in the gaps between the tubes.

In 2007, Finnish company Artek commissioned Ban to build its Milan furniture fair pavilion, which he fabricated from a paper and plastic composite produced by UPM and made from recycled, and sustainable, self-adhesive labelling materials. In 2009, he used this same composite to reproduce one of his few industrial designs, also for Artek: Ban originally introduced his L-Unit System in 1993, which consisted of L-shaped wood-scrap units joined modularly to compose a limitless array of chairs, benches and tables. Once again, the use of a single repeatable module allows flat-packing for easy storage and transport while holes pre-cut in each provide joint connections but minimize the object's weight. The architect has worked in other materials to make furniture (his *Tenax* chair, shown at the Tokyo Fibre exhibit, featured a super-slender 25 mm carbon fibre profile derived from acrylonitrile), but his is a body of work that makes one hope that Ban will always remain a paper designer, in every sense of the phrase.

2009
One Chair is Enough Exhbition
Producer: Artek

SHIGERU BAN

1

2

3

DIANE STEVERLYNCK

2008
1 Tight Stool
Material: Ash wood, PES braid
Producer: © 2009 Trico International

The seat and legs of Steverlynck's stool are bound together by the incidental and cheerful ornamental thread wound round its waist.

PHILIPPE NIGRO

2009
2 Twin Chair
Material: Wood, plastic
Photography: VIA / Marie Flores
Producer: VIA / Valorisation de l'Innovation dans l'Ameublement

4 Pietement Table
Material: Wood, metal
Producer: Producer: VIA / Valorisation de l'Innovation dans l'Ameublement

SALOMÉ DE FONTAINIEU & GODEFROY DE VIRIEU

2009
3 Lamellé-Décolé Chair
Material: Wood, plastic
Photography: S. de Fonainieu & G. de Virieu
Producer: VIA / Valorisation de l'Innovation dans l'Ameublement

ELLENBERGERDESIGN STUDIO
Jannis Ellenberger

2009
5 Bench
Photography: Alexander Fanslau

4

5

STONE DESIGN

2008
1 PALET SOFA
Material: Polyurethane foam,
upholstery fabric, wood
Producer: Goher

2009
2 FIELDS SOFA
Material: Polyurethane foam,
upholstery fabric, synthetic leather
Producer: RS

HARRI KOSKINEN WORKS
Harri Koskinen

2000/2009 re-edition
3 Sofabed
Producer: Harri Koskinen Works

1

2

3

1

STUDIO MAKKINK & BEY
Rianne Makkink & Jurgen Bey

2009
1 Ear Chair
Producer: Prooff

2009
2 The Work Sofa
Producer: Prooff

2

1

2

FORMFORYOU

2009

1 **Kiter Armchair**
Material: Upholstered seat and backrest
with plywood frame
Photography: André Löfgren
Producer: formforyou

ADRIEN ROVERO

2009

2 **Flip Sofa/Table**
Material: Metal, foam, textile, wood
Producer: Campeggi

Flip comprises a board and two trestles and
can serve either as an improvised writing
table or couch.

TOKUJIN YOSHIOKA

3 **Heaven Chair**
Photography: Nicola Zocchi
Producer: Cassina

GREIGE
Daniel Lorch

2008

4 **Marshmallow Chair**
Material: Rubber foam, linen, steel tube

3

4

Thank the motorcycle for putting the brakes on British designer Tom Dixon's music career and launching him – via the hospital with two broken bones – into industrial design. After dropping out of London's Chelsea Art School, Dixon took up welding for the sake of motorcycle maintenance and began to play with industrial scrap and sheet metal to make sculpture and sculptural furniture. The tools, themselves – gauges, guillotines, arc, tig and mig welders – sometimes determined the form and construction of these early pieces.

New Spot Table (2009)

By the mid-1980's, Cappellini produced Dixon's woven S chair and the engineered-looking Pylon table and chair. A decade later, Dixon had moved on to plastics, founding the lighting company Eurolounge before becoming creative director of Terence Conran's Habitat. He finally founded his own studio and began to art-direct Finland's Alvar Aalto legacy firm, Artek.

Instead of music, the self-taught designer has been playing with tools, structure, form, materials, efficient product distribution, interior design and colour since the beginning. Over time, he has also proven himself a master of self-promotion, a champion of sustainable design and an inventive businessman. Within seven minutes, during the 2006 London Design Festival, Dixon gave away 500 Expanded Polystyrene chairs in Trafalgar Square. (To finance this seeming commercial heedlessness, he sold several versions plated with pure copper in the form of a micron-thick vacuum-metalized film through New York's Moss Gallery.) During the subsequent London design fair, he gave away 1000 energy-saving lamps. In front of a live audience at Art Basel / Design Miami that same year, Dixon extruded clear plastic into thick ropy cables and wove them into his *Fresh Fat Easy Chair*. Under his direction, Artek has begun tagging historical Aalto chairs with radio frequency identification (RFID) chips that record the ongoing life story of each chair, allowing new owners to add the latest instalment of the narrative.

In 2008, Dixon established an in-house interior design studio that dashingly kitted out the interiors of the Shoreditch House and Century Club in London. The designer's latest *Utility* collection featured pressed glass lighting, stone and vitreous enamel tables – chunky industrial or natural materials translated into fresh, shapely pieces that hold up weight and durability as virtues because they represent the longevity of the object – the first, forgotten quality of sustainability. Happily, Dixon revisits successful former pieces regularly. He's done so with his glamorous globe lights, creating blow-moulded polycarbonate pendants with white interiors and shocking matte fluorescent exteriors. They recall the use of "safety" colours in emergency equipment and act as a source of brilliance even when the light is turned off in your room or in your head.

tomdixon.net, designresearchstudio.net

2009
New Block Table

TOM DIXON

2008
Upholstery Collection

ATELIER JACOB
Marco Jacob

2009
1 Chapi Chapo Hoop Chair
  Material: Powder-coated steel
  Photography: Miguel Jacob
  Producer: Atelier Jacob / PD Lab

KORBAN / FLAUBERT

2008
2 Jetstream Bench
  Material: Stainless steel
  Photography: KORBAN/FLAUBERT
  Producer: KORBAN/FLAUBERT

BENGTSSON DESIGN LTD
Mathias Bengtsson

2004
3 Spun Round Chair
  Material: Carbon fiber
  Photography: Martin Scott Jupp
  Producer: Bengtsson design ltd

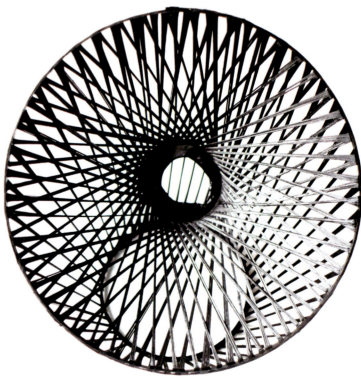

2008
Discarded Hanger and FRP Shell Chair
Material: Discarded Hanger & Discarded FRP shell chair
Photography : HATTA

Shell is made from discarded wire hangers and an FRP stadium chair designed by Isamu Kenmochi for use in baseball stadiums and railway stations. Because they are not recyclable or suitable for incineration, they generate tons of waste at the end of their lifecycle. Nosigner pays homage to the Eames' *Shell Chair Eiffel Base*, which in turn inspired Kenmochi's stadium chair.

ERNESTO OROZA

2001/2007 re-edition
1 Provisional Bench
Material: Metal bars, wood and Formica
Photography: Ernesto Oroza
Producer: Ernesto Oroza

OSKO + DEICHMANN

2009
2 Straw Chair

The bent tube has served as a symbol for modernity in furniture design. Today, as Bauhaus approaches its 100th year, the *Straw Chair* brings an innovation to tubular steel furniture: the kinked tube. "Some might call it blasphemy," the designers say. "We call it reformation."

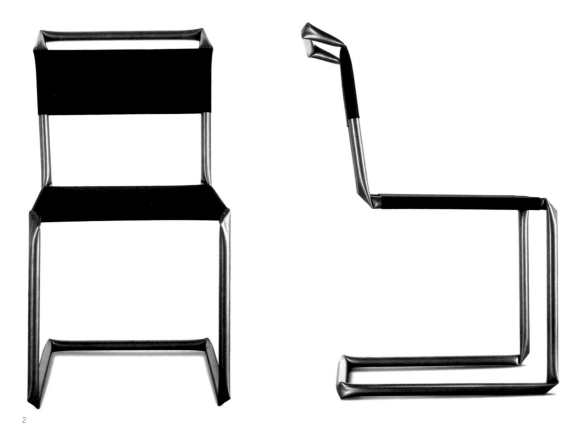

2

2008
Alieno Chair
Material: Metal
Producer: Casamania

The term "alien" derives from the Latin "al-
ius" which means "other." The design is intended to put a friendly face on the diversity
of the other.

Master of the fractal, if not the entire universe, Arik Levy has fascinated us with his own fascination for natural phenomena: meteors, minerals and metaphors with an earthy provenance. Disdaining the old dichotomies that once divided technology from Mother Nature, engineering from art, and space from spirit, Levy's polished, nearly Platonic products for clients like Swarovski, Vitra and Chicago's Wright20 Gallery, move easily between showroom and art space.

With names like *Fluid* (shelves), *Fire* (coffee tables), *Gaia* (an armchair) and *Geological Landscape* (also shelving), is it really that difficult to divine the designer's inspiration? His *Fuse Rock* benches, the *Meteor Light* for Serralunga and the creased *Rockmirror* are enlightened (sometimes literally) studies of their subjects. The *Fractal Light* series weaves together hundreds or, in one case, even thousands of slender clusters of micro-fluorescent light tubes to create a single light-emitting "textile," a diffuse precipitation of illumination.

For Swarovski's pared-down 2009 Milan exhibition, the designer riffed on facets of a variety of materials with thick wire-form pendant lights, a softly upholstered but sharply crystalline reading "cave" and a redux of *Meteor* in the form of stackable magnetic toys. Levy's shelving for E15 and his *Beam* table for Swedese translate the mineral power of his forms into wood with *Beam* extracting –a staple component of architecture– inserting it into a new (still load-bearing) context.

Just as architectural if more meditatively refined, Levy's series of stacked glass vases and his sheer-layered candelabra for Gaia&Gino draw the gaze ineluctably through the object (the absorption of the object by the eye is delayed by microseconds as one is forced to follow the lines of the object's edges or reflections, one can't do both). Their appearance

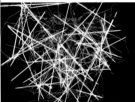

Fractal Cloud (2007)

also seems to change radically depending on the choice to produce them with a particular material or finish . The see-through cylinders of the glass candleholders offer soft layers that can be penetrated, while the same piece produced in silver seems to have an entirely new form, depth and mood. A translucent honeycombed 3D-printed fruit bowl for Materialise .MGX actually recalls the warm glow of beeswax. This respectful but imaginative approach to materials, form and production technique tends to make solid, inanimate objects appear as mercurial as wind and water.

Born in Tel Aviv in 1963, Levy earned a degree from the Swiss Art Centre College of Design and settled in Paris where he created stage sets for modern dance performances before co-founding the Ldesign Group in 1997 with Pippo Lionni. The studio turns out everything from corporate identities to interiors and exhibitions, from tabletop, furniture and lighting – to a windbreaker for Kolon Sport. This prolific output encompasses some masterful pieces: pivot the weighted ends of Levy's balletic silver *Balance* candleholder for Gaia&Gino, and you can use the other end as a vase. This piece provides a fine illustration of Levy's mechanical pragmatism which, taken to its extreme, becomes poetic. It is a body of work that reminds us that humans can, indeed, become a force majeure – in a good way – if we only want.

www.ariklevy.fr

1

2008
1 **Absent Nature Exhibition**
   Producer: Wright20 Gallery

2009
2 **Wedge Table**
   Material: Chinese green and black granite
   Producer: Cesare Chimenti

2009
3 **Arie Shelving**
   Producer: E15

ARIK LEVY

2

3

From Recessionista to Pure Form Sublime

83

RAIMUND PUTS

2009
1 Raimund Light
Producer: Moooi

DRIFT
Lonneke Gordijn and Ralph Nauta

2009
2 Shylight
Material: Plexiglass, RVS, Silk
Photography: Ralph Nauta
Producer: DRIFT

Shylight is a lamp hidden in a cocoon and based on the natural process by which flowers attract and repel pollen-gathering bees. Whenever the lamp is switched on, it falls out of its "cocoon," opens its petals and floats downward. When switched off, it closes again. Drift have exploited highly technical electronic solutions in order to create a poetic and 'living' luminaire. Every lamp is programmable by its user and can be combined with additional *Shylights* to perform a "dance" of shifting, dimming illumination.

1

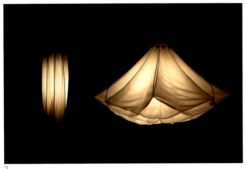

2

1

JARROD LIM DESIGN
Jarrod Lim

2009
1 Koi Chair
Material: Steel, wood
3 Doppler Lamp
Material: Aluminium, electrical components
Photography: Jarrod Lim
Producer: Jarrod Lim

HARRI KOSKINEN

2008
2 Substance Chair
Producer: Fornasarig

2

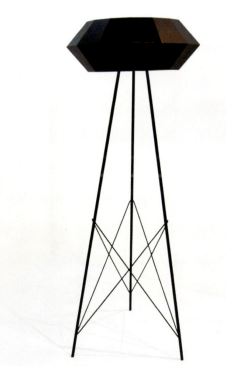

3

From Recessionista to Pure Form Sublime

Performing Arts and Crafts

The long and fruitful relationship between art and design is characterised by differing phases of convergence and demarcation, —————————————————————

———————————————— by mutual inspiration and the processing of results particular to each discipline using techniques and possibilities borrowed from the other.

Logo Studio (2008)

The work of Donald Judd would be impossible to imagine without classic modernism in design, while the contemporary installations of Damien Hirst and Takashi Murakami would scarcely make sense as public provocation in a design context. But the design discipline's current shift towards the field of art draws its inspiration from another epoch. The social conscience rooted within design was searching for a kindred spirit in art and finally unearthed the idea of social sculpture. This milestone of conceptual art – developed in the 1960s by the German artist Joseph Beuys – no longer restricts the definition of art to the physical artwork itself, but expands the notion to include a further intangible level. According to Beuys, it is specifically about the transformative social impact of creative action and how sculptural work can produce it. But not only that: the theory of social sculpture defines absolutely everyone as being an artist, capable of contributing his/her own creativity to the common good and therefore able to help in the broadest sense with actively shaping society. No particular artistic skills are required. Beuys believed that the necessary abilities for creating a social sculpture were openness, spirituality and imagination. Abilities, in other words, that already exist in every human being and need only to be unlocked and nurtured.

Mia Hamborg (2009)

It's all about context and process.

At the heart of the social sculpture idea is the human being whose creative abilities make him/her capable of developing social structures and contexts. This development should be understood as a continuous creative process. The concept of social sculpture can be described as social action – activities that positively influence the overall good of society – combined with the idea of sculpture as involving a mouldable and shapeable object that provides a visual, haptic, acoustic or thermal experience. In contrast to the conventional, formal aesthetic definition of art, social sculpture's more anthropological approach to art encompasses any type of creative human activity. Every-thing designed and produced by a human being using his/her own creativity defines him/her as being the sole force that can actively transform society and its contexts. Building on this theory, art is no longer restricted to material artefacts presented to a relatively small public in a museum. Rather it permeates the whole of society in order to replace obsolete ways of life with new forms in

Bram Boo (2009)

every possible area. But this places social sculpture close to the social notion of design that was formulated as an ideal during the first half of the 20th century: by permeating society with objects that are useful, functional and aesthetic, society can be transformed in the sense of attaining a different (i.e. better) quality of life.

Processing experience

The assumption that everyone possesses the creativity to actively shape their own environment has since become one of the cornerstones of a marketing theory that depicts the creative consumer integrated within the organic process of his/her entire product world. For the consumer, assembling a piece of furniture can metamorphose into the ultimate discovery of his/her own capabilities. It offers physical self-experience as a kind of therapy in an increasingly disembodied world. And there are now a whole range of interesting therapies available for these emotional conditions. Designers are developing innovative blueprints and casually revolutionising the somewhat outdated DIY store along the way. With simple but intelligent designs, the familiar limitations of self-buildable furniture are being exploited. The process of assembly is becoming a satisfying experience. Innovative details and unusual material compositions add to the aesthetic spectrum. And that is not all: in the actual process of putting it together, the furniture becomes human and profoundly democratic. What emerges, with the designer and user now on equal terms, is social sculpture in the best possible sense.

Max Lamb (2008)

Fluxus furniture

Design's current interest in a socially-oriented definition of art is also apparent in the temporary loaning of certain formal aspects. Design that is process-like and unfinished, produced in collectives, provisional and fleeting – hallmarks of so much contemporary work – appears to have been borrowed from the pool of techniques cultivated by conceptual art. Movements from the 1960s such as Fluxus and happenings seem to have lost none of their topicality, except that now the focal point can be something as profane as furniture being dismantled and then put back together again in an ongoing installation. What unites the conceptual art of the past with the conceptual design of today is the reference to the old master Marcel Duchamp. Duchamp tore the everyday object out if its social context and presented it within the museum setting as a work of art.

Nacho Carbonell (2009)

Fluxus then released this everyday art from the museum and criticised Duchamp's approach for relying on the established definition of art in order to differentiate his own anti-art. Fluxus dissolved the polarisation by ultimately declaring both everything and nothing to be art – a theory which, given the complete transformation of the social context over the past two decades, can be seamlessly extended to design. Today, the site for presenting and using a design object is no longer confined to the apartment or the office. It could just as easily be a gallery or an auction house. And it could equally be the place where the design object is produced, because what the object represents does not necessarily have to be regarded as a finished work. And apart from the designer, the object's users can actively help to complete the work in their own fashion.

Karen Ryan (2009)

Democratic green

In the theory of social sculpture, every human being is granted the personal freedom to operate in society as an individual. But within this matrix of possibilities, he/she also feels responsible towards society as a whole. The work of each individual on the social sculpture unifies the various different groups within society, making it an expedient force for solving their problems – social, economic or ecological – through creative structuring and shared responsibility. Thus the idea of the social sculpture is driven by the hope – especially pertinent in view of growing ecological challenges – that art can mediate between man and the environment and thereby change life on our planet for the better. It is hardly surprising that this romantic approach to tackling our environmental problems was adapted by design. Those designers who are currently dealing with ecological questions are consciously looking for a collective and process-oriented context in which to manifest their individual responsibility towards society. As artists or designers in the spirit of social sculpture, they do not subscribe to the theories of the early ecological movements in design such as that of product avoidance or usage rather than ownership. Rather they want to design new and innovative things – precisely as if the productive creativity that Beuys called for was the panacea for achieving positive changes in society. Their key issue is recycling – the idea of the creative reuse of industrial society's waste and the participation of broad social strata in the production process of their own sculptures. Production here takes place largely outside the industrial framework. The agenda is much more about the process of craftsmanship and artisan manufacturing. The

Scrap Lab (2008)

greater the opportunity for an individual to exert an active influence on the end product through his/her own abilities, the higher that object will be valued: it is the result of a collective democratic process. And because climate change and environmental devastation ultimately represent an existential threat in this age of the globalised economy – one that affects everyone in equal measure – it is the goal of social sculpture to redistribute the production process throughout the entire world. Thanks to the united efforts of designers and producers on social sculpture – in our case a design object – the social differences between them are overcome.

Tokujin Yoshioka (2009)

CHRISTIAN HALLERÖD
Christian Halleröd and Johannes Svartholm

2008
Mobile Mobile Office & Art
Material : Steel, wood
Producer: Mossutställningar

Mobile is a furniture installation created by artists Christian Halleröd and Johannes Svartholm for non-profit arts company Mossutställningar and featured in the touring exhibition called Los Angeles by French artist Sophie Calle. The designers developed a structure that expressed mobility and flexibility while providing a consistent, easily recognizable image for the organization.

Mossutställningar was founded with the goal of making Stockholm a more open city, with art-filled public spaces, whether street or fine art where unexpected interactions could occur among creative community and other inhabitants. Halleröd and Svartholm were commissioned early on to find a flexible form, within which the non-profit could function and present itself to the public in a variety of contexts: in the middle of a square, on a lake, on TV or at a dumpsite. Although the furniture has a strong graphical presence it is suitable to any context and remains flexible enough to accommodate Mossutställningar's future expansion goals.

Mobile's unique, sculptural modules borrow from traditional office space archetypes, but disperse these throughout the frame. Each of the four units may be used separately or in combination to create micro-architectural variations: a room, partitions, a stage, complex sculptural structures or even labyrinths.

GITTA GSCHWENDTNER

2008
Bag Stool
Material: Woodcrete
Photography: Luke Hayes

Design Museum and *Time Out* magazine commissioned Gitta Gschwendtner to investigate the connection between design and the city through an installation for the Design Museum Tank exploring the theme "Consume." As a metaphor for material consumption, Gschwendtner made woodcrete stools from an ecofriendly and lightweight mixture of concrete and wood fibre, and then cast each piece from moulds based on paper shopping bags. Their irregular forms were generated during the casting process. The stools provide the visitor with a place to sit and experience a contemplative moment with a view of London that presents an alternative to, say, shopping.

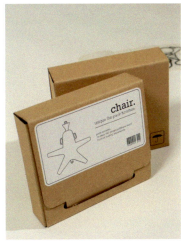

ADAM PATERSON

2008
Chair
Material: Concrete
Photography: Lawrence Lee

Paterson presents a new take on "flat-pack" furniture that draws the user into the production process. After buying a kit containing a clear 480-gauge polyethelene mold, the user may choose the ingredients that will go into the concrete that will harden into their unique chair: mix, pour, position and wait...

It's all about Context and Process

BRAM BOO

2009
1 Desk Overdose
2 Chair Overdose
    Material: Lacqered MDF and wood
    Photography: Jasper Willemen
    Producer: Bram Boo

A desk and chair with storage units dispersed
in a nonchalant way, giving the user endless
opportunities to create order from disorder.

1

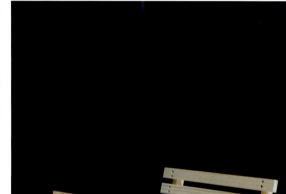

MAX LAMB

2008
DIY Chair
Material: Pine or other
softwoods and
zinc-plated screws

LOGO STUDIO
Gean Moreno and Ernesto Oroza

2008
Studio Scrap Stool
Material: Wood
Photography: Ernesto Oroza 2008
Producer: Logo Studio

1

2

3

4

5

6

7

8

9

10

GODSPEED

2008
1 **Stick Chair**
2 **Bouquet Dinner Table**
3 **Bouquet High Table**
   Material: Wood, screws
4 **Three and a Half Pallets**
   Material: Pallets

2009
5 **Stick Chair with Planks**
6 **Färgfabriken**
   Material: Wood, screws

2008
7 **Lighting at Nr. 4**
   Material: Wood, tape
8 **Nr. 4**
   Material: Paper, glue
9 **Nr. 4**
10 **Nr. 4**
   Material: Wood, screws

SIBYLLE STŒCKLI

2008
The Crate
Material: Wood board, Auro paint, staples
Photography: Pénélope Henriod

A crate is a basic, standardised object. When the shape is altered slightly, our perception of it can change radically.

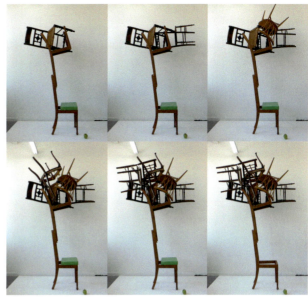

KAREN RYAN

2009
1 **In The Woods Chair**
Material: Discarded
wooden chairs
Photography: Karen Ryan

2008
2 **Wood Work Light Sculpture**
Material: Off-cuts of wood, acrylic
discarded by other designers
Photography: Karen Ryan
Client: Rossana Orlandi

In The Woods is a tree for the living room, and a piece of seating, made from salvaged chairs. The British designer's choice to use discarded objects and materials in her work is a political and personal one, a response to increasing consumer waste as well as the artist's own limited resources. Ryan hunts for and gathers her materials locally in her home city of Portsmouth.

"Unstructured structures, lit externally," as Ryan describes them. Made from scraps gathered from the waste thrown out by other designers, the pieces contain "the negatives" of others' work and introduce viewers to the beauty of the byproduct.

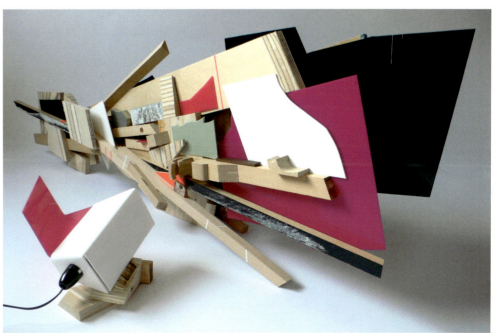

CHRISTOFFER ANGELL

2009
1 Beehive Chair
Material: Cast polyurethane
Photography: Mads Hårstad Pålsrud

As its name suggests, this chair was inspired by bees: industrious creatures that use space and materials to optimal effect. The honeycomb's hexagon offers strength, space-efficiency and a minimal use of materials. "I wanted to design a crystal-clear example of my views about using as few resources as possible in a design process," Angell explains.

ALON MERON

2008
2 Endoskeleton Domestic Landscape
Material: Wood, foam, wool, steel
Photography: Alon Meron
Producer: Alon Meron

Humans deeply associate comfort and safety with containment, a fact widely demonstrated by the character of our domestic architecture and interiors. Our houses are rigid shells in which we choreograph our daily lives, letting our movements flow from one room to the other. Based on the endo- and exoskeletons that support the human body, Meron's latest work explores our notions of shelter.

ARCHITETTURA ROCK
Niki Makariou

2009
3 YiaYia Chair
Material: Wood/wool
Photography: bookhou
Producer: bookhou

The mixture of wood and yarn combines the silkiness, warmth and tenderness of the yarn and the stateliness, durability and simplicity of the wood. This combination of materials and feelings reminds me my grandmother sitting on her wooden chair while knitting. With this picture in my mind I decided to create the *YiaYia chair*. *YiaYia* in Greek means grandmother. The idea of creating this design made me understand that there is no need to throw or give away our old furniture as we can always renovate them and create something new and bizarre.

PETER ANDERSSON

2007
4 Set Piece Armchair
Material: Pine, leather
Photography: 20ltd
Project Assistant: Patrik Bengtsson
Producer: The studio

On first inspection, it appears like a functional chair – impeccably handcrafted in white leather. But look a little further and its true excitement and originality is revealed. *Set Piece* is minimalism taken to an ironic extreme; it is also study in construction, a revelation behind the polished exterior – reminiscent of a glimpse of the wings of a theatre or a movie set.

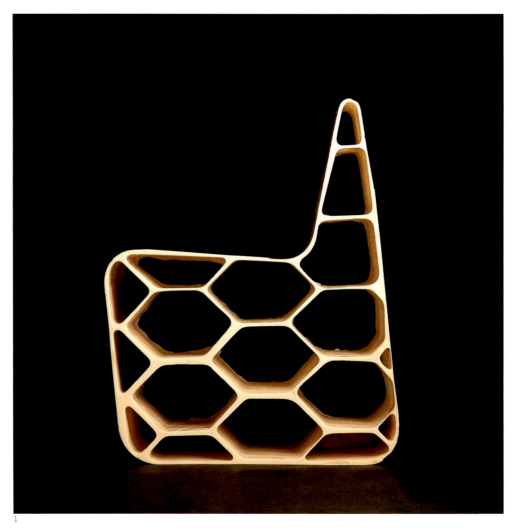

1

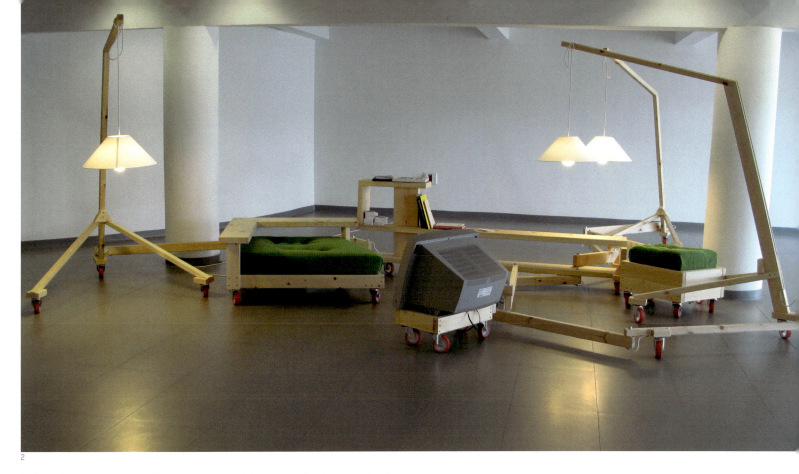

2

3

4

HUNN WAI

2009
PING-PONG Dining Table
Material: Dupont Corian, gold lacquer, oak
Art Direction: Francesca Lanzavecchia
Photography: Daniel Peh K.L., *www.rexice.com*
Producer: Mein Gallery

A dining table that recalls the origins of table-tennis in the form of a table suited to both dining and mano-a-mano racquet sports. What started off as impromptu after-dinner amusement mimicking tennis in an indoor upper class Victorian environment became an international phenomenon with rules and standards. This product is an official-sized game table with a Dupont Corian surface CNC-routed with French Rococo patterns and ping-pong iconography, filled with gold lacquer, supported by stately hand-lathed timber legs. At its center, a long rectangular vase filled with flowers serves as a net and a centerpiece. *Ping-pong*, the table, uses a high-tech and thoroughly modern marble-like material (Corian) while emphasizing grandeur and pomp through its neo-classical embellishments.

1

2

3

PETER SCHÄFER

2008
1 **Ad Hoc #15**
Material: Mixed media

2007
2 **Ad Hoc #09**
Material: Mixed media

2009
3 **Ad Hoc #17**
Material: Mixed media
Producer: KKAARRLLS

"Find ways in which you are not controlled by your furniture," urges designer Peter Schäfer. Through his constructions, Schäfer wants us to discover how to use our furniture in the precise, and shifting, ways that we – not the designer or manufacturer – want. Pulling furniture from its context, he creates a semifinished product for spontaneously and continuously composing fresh, perfectly personal, domestic environments.

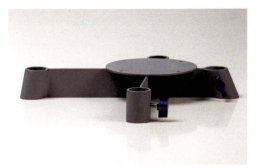

THE GREEN HOUSE ARCHITECTS
Niklas Madsen/Per Eriksson

2009
RCO Chair
Material: Steel,wood, felt
Photography: Fredrik Segerfalk

Designers today are bringing Do It Yourself and customization to a whole new level. Green House envisions this chair's manufacturer making only the mechanism to bind the pieces of a chair together, allowing the user to supply the rest of the materials – seat, back, legs – as they see fit. Discarded furniture elements or even items unrelated to a chair could become a part of this new seating collage.

DANIEL ROHR

2007
Screw Table Clamp Table
Material: Aluminium, acryl glass
Producer: Daniel Rohr

Due to its multifunctional attributes, the use of screw clamps, whose brackets are pressed onto a workpiece by a screw spindle, enables extended utilization e.g. design of a new furniture aesthetic. The idea centers around screw clamps being used as functional - and design objects.

DESIGNASYL

2008

1 Stay at My Home Furniture Set for Guests
Material: Viscoelastic foam, cold-cure foam, waterproof
textile, padding, lacquered MDF, PMMA, LEDs, electronics,
battery, wool felt, sateen
Photography: Rebecca Sulista

This series of objects enables hosts to set up a comfortable environment for overnight guests. Lightweight objects
simplify the experience of offering hospitality, the designer
suggests, "a very important virtue in a globalised world."

LLOT LLOV

2008

2 Matt Light
Photography: Khrystell Zavaleta

Matt is a lighting element with the capacity to dynamically adapt
itself to the individual needs of its user, changing its appearance
according to the site of its installation.

3 Ray Light
Material: Knitwear
Photography: llot llov
Producer: llot llov - artwork shop

Ray is a puppy-like lamp that can follow its owner. The cable of
this hanging light is over 12 metres, enabling *Ray* to become a
floor, pendant, or atmospheric luminairy.

2

3

1

LLOT LLOV

2009

1 Clark Desk
   Material: Lacquered MDF
   Photography: *www.fotografie-lucie-eisenmann.de*

Clark provides temporary storage via vertical stacking instead of filing or sorting. Everything stays within arm's reach and does not disappear into drawers or cupboards. Clark acknowledges the most common ways of storing oft-used objects in our work-space and extrapolates from these quotidien habits in a variety of ways.

ZOË MOWAT

2007

2 Desk Buddy Organizer
   Material: Cherry wood off-cuts, industrial felt
   Photography: Zoë Mowat

This handsome office companion is a simple and adaptable object intended to neatly organize pencils, erasers, paperclips and other tools of the desktop.

OD-DO ARHITEKTI

2008

3 Landscape Carpet
   Material: Waterproof textile, EPS granules
   Photography: od-do

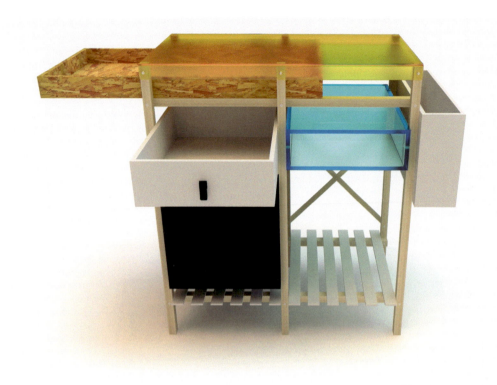

1

CHRISTIAN VIVANCO

2009

1 From a Lost City Multiuse Furniture
Material: Wood, MMA, OSB
Photography: Christian Vivanco

Inspired by the irregular and ad hoc character of the shantytowns and favelas of South America, *FALC* preserves the virtues of improvisational and resourceful living, while celebrating the absence of the grid and the freedom of disorder. This furniture can be used as storage, work surface, or kitchen accessory.

JACK BRANDSMA

2007

2 RestRuimte/SpareSpace
Material: Poplar plywood, waxed steel tubes
Photography: Sabina Theijs,
info@sabinatheijs.com
Producer: Een paar ontwerpers
(A pair of designers)

For the SpareSpace Foundation, Jack Brandsma designed a set of mobile units including four desks, a table, cupboard and a bar. With this micro-architectural kit, every empty space can be transformed into a temporary office. The pilot project is still set up in an empty shop in Groningen, The Netherlands by a few start-up entrepeneurs in the creative industry.

2

1

2

3

4

5

6

PUNGA AND SMITH

2007
1 Sacrificial Chair Garment Rack
Material: Powdercoated mild steel
Photography: Stephen Goodenough

A reaction to the habit of shedding clothes in every direction possible at the end of the day, rendering the nearest chair "useless." Or is it?

LLOT LLOV

2009
2 Todd Laundry Stool
Material: Steel
Photography: Lucie Eisenmann,
www.fotografie-lucie-eisenmann.de

2008
5 Wannabe Table
Material: Cardboard
Photography: Lucie Eisenmann,
Producer: Pulpo

CHRISTIAN LESSING

2008
3 Collecteur Magazine Rack Stool
Material: Painted steel, removable cushion
Photography: Claudia Rath
Producer: Lessing Produktgestaltung

TOM PRICE

2008
4 Fleece Chair: Fur
Material: Discarded polyester clothing
Photography: Christoph Bolten

MARTÌ GUIXE

2009
6 Xarxa Sofa
Material: Multilayer birch, painted metal rod, cotton, linen, viscose and polyester
Photography: Federico Villa
Producer: Danese Milano

Processing Experience
111

SCHEMA ARCHITECTURE OFFICE
Jo Nagasaka

2009
Paco Holiday House
Photography: NACASA&PARTNERS
Producer: ROOVICE

Paco is three-meter-square vacation house, 80% factory-assembled and delivered to its site by a car – like a piece of furniture.

3

1

MICHAEL SCHONER

2008
1 Boombench
Material: Multiplex and stainless steel, sound system
Photography: Michael Schoner
Producer: 2D&W, Amsterdam

HARCO RUTGERS

2007
2 Rockin' Chair
Material: Multiplex, plastic foam foil, contact microphones, effects processor, headphone amplifier
Photography: Harco Rutgers
Producer: Harco Rutgers

This rocking chair comes equipped with two sensitive contact microphones so that even the slightest tremor in the chair is amplified through the headphones. Fiddle with the knobs on the versatile effects processor and learn how to control the chair's audio output. Originally designed for individual use, with headphones, it now is also booked regularly for live performances in combination with renowned percussionists, and amplified through a PA system.

ARCHITETTURA ROCK
Su Hyun Lee

2009
3 C/F11110011 Modular Musical Chair

C/F11110011 takes its cues from electronic music which is created by editing digital sounds. Likewise, the *C/F11110011* is "edited" by combining electronic components into an electronic circuit that allows any device to be plugged in. Various accessories can be connected and disconnected to "remix" different versions of this furniture experience.

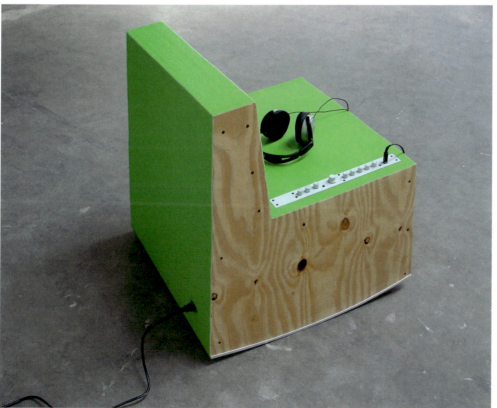

2

2008
RGB Floor Lamp
Producer: ZERO lightning

FREDRIK MATTSON

2007
PXL Pendant Lamp
Material: Aluminium
Producer: ZERO lightning

MIA HAMBORG

2009
Stacking Table
Material: Spray-painted wood
Photography: Martin Gustavsson

A colourful table that the user may customize just as they might bead a necklace. An inventive, modular way to apply the beauty and craft of lathe-turned objects.

SEBASTIAN BRAJKOVIC

2008
1 Lathe Chair VIII

2009
2 Lathe Chair III
3 Lathe Chair IV/V
4 Lathe Chair II
5 Lathe Chair I
   Material: Bronze, embroidered fabric
   Photography: Sebastian Brajkovic and
   Carpenters Workshop Gallery
   Producer: Sebastian Brajkovic

Lathe chairs seem to turn on a central axis. These versions of lathe-turned seating are fabricated in a completely artisanal way, but inspired by and designed on the computer. They suggest a story that is both old and brand new, and honor the creativity of days both before and after the digital era. The chairs are part of the permanent collection of London's Victoria and Albert Museum.

2

3

1

4

5

1

2

3

KAI LINKE

2009
1 Mirror Chair No.4
2 Mirror Chair No.3
3 Mirror Chair No.2
4 Mirror Chair No.1
Material: Polypropylene
Photography: Kai Linke

4

MAARTEN DE CEULAER

2006
1 Contrast Chair
Material: Plexiglass, transparent stickers

By sticking views of a classical wooden chair onto a basic Plexi seat, the designer created a hologram-effect while playing with old and new forms and materials.

2009
2 Rubber Iron Book Ends
Material: Polyurethane

2007
3 My Childhood Memories Chair
Material: Toys

2008
4 A Pile of Suitcases Closet and Luggage
Material: Multiplex, hardboard, leather
Photography: Astrid Zuidema
Producer: Nilufar Gallery (Milan)

VALENTINA GONZALEZ WOHLERS

2009

1 Prickly Pair Chairs
Material: Carved wood & upholstery (Viscose and linen)
Woodworks: J.K. Bone.
Upholstery: BC Upholstery Ltd
Photography:VolkerKetteniss, *volker.ketteniss@WGSN.com*
Producer: Valentina Gonzalez Wohlers

A furniture project conceived from the creative experience of a Mexican designer in Europe. *The Prickly pair chairs* combines the distinctive formal and aesthetical values behind Mexican and European figurative idiosyncrasy resulting in a furniture object within which both cultures are identified. It is at once frivolous and humorous yet in the same moment encourages reflection and acceptance. Shapes, materials, colours, textures and finishes collide in irreverent and playful harmony; the *Prickly pair chairs* is a statement against prejudgements and preconceptions.

1

SIBYLLE STŒCKLI

2008

2 Sofa Hermann R.
Material: Wood, foam, Kvadrat 100% biocotton
Photography: Michel Bonvin
Cover sewn by Cornelia Peter,
www.petermuellerfashion.com

Hermann offers multiple ways of reclining. Users can sit on two sides if the "back" is placed in the middle of its seat, choose a low or high back, or remove it entirely to create an extra double bed.

2008

3 Modular Soft Bags Seating
Material: Cotton, Gor-Tex©, polystyrene balls
Photography: Pénélope Henriod
With the help of Mover Sportswear and the
Ikea Swiss Foundation

2

3

Fluxus Furniture

1

2

NACHO CARBONELL

2009
1 **Table / Skin Collection**
2 **Table+1 / Skin Collection**
3 **Table+2 / Skin collection**
   Material: Fiber, rubber
   Photography: Studio Nacho Carbonell
   Producer: Nacho Carbonell

The *Skin Collection* allows users to place objects beneath a thin, closely adhering elastic layer that sheathes each surface. This layer takes the form of the objects, creating contours that pique the curiosity. Carbonell chose the un-conventional leg heights with the intention of changing the user's perspective.

3

REDDISH STUDIO

2008
1 **Dov Tables and Stools**
Material: Cast aluminum
Photography: Dan Lev
Producer: Reddish studio

The starting point of each piece is a block of polystyrene. By incorporating hand-work into the process, the material's native qualities were used to generate endless variations on the theme.

ASIF KHAN

2009
2 **BBchair**
Material: Moulded plastic spheres
Photography: Asif Khan

BBchair was moulded from small plastic spheres and formed in a one-step process. Natural variations in the packaging of the balls brings uniqueness to an otherwise industrial process. Each version of the chair shows its personality through imperfections incidental to its production.

1

PETER MACAPIA

2008

1 HammerNSong Double Stool
Material: Duraform SLS process
Photography: Peter Macapia
Producer: Peter Macapia

2007

2 Xstool Laocoön
Photography: Peter Macapia
Producer: Johnson Trading Gallery

Though organic-looking, these *stool*s were developed through complex digital explorations of form, viscocity and surface tension, which generated a porous, ossified appearance.

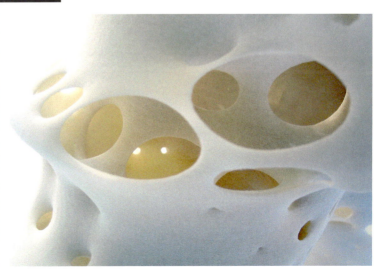

2

1

PEPE HEYKOOP

2008

1 Liquid Pillows Chair
Material: Wood, polyurethane, rubber
Photography: Pepe Heykoop
Producer: Studio Pepe Heykoop

Heykoop dripped foam over the frame of a rigid wooden chair and then sealed the layers with a coat of rubber.

LUKA STEPAN DESIGN

2008

2 Grown Chair
Material: Laser-sintered plastic

Stepan sought to "grow" objects in the computer and create a direct relation between these objects and rapid manufacturing technologies. This led to the design of the actual digital process in addition to the objects, themselves, rather than using existing CAD software.

2

1

2

LUKA STEPAN DESIGN

2007
2 0.01 Sec Vases
Material: Laser-sintered nylon
Photography: Baruch Natah
Producer: Ronen Kadushin

With fluid simulation software typically used in the Hollywood special effects industry, Stepan captured the shape of water flowing into a vessel every one-hundredth of a second (along with absent form of the original vessel). The 3D data representing favourite frames in the sequence (700 in total) was then printed via an SLS (selective laser sintering) rapid-prototyping machine.

RONEN KADUSHIN

2001
1 Discast Chair
Material: Cast aluminum
Photography: Baruch Natah
Producer: Ronen Kadushin

Kadushin stuck pieces of wood into a sandbox and then poured molten aluminum into the cavities left behind when the sticks were removed. The resulting chair was made in two parts. Bulges at the foot of the front legs were produced when the sand "sponged in" the aluminum.

1

DAG DESIGNLAB

2008
1 Negev Low Table
Material: Plastic
Photography: Yonatan Bossidan
Producer: DAG-designlab

KWANGHO LEE

2008
2 Cioccolato Bianco Sofa
Material: Styrofoam
Photography: Kwangho Lee
Producer: Kwangho Lee

Part of the designer's study of raw materials. Lee focused on the possiblilties of creating innovative forms and creating a new role for an ubiquitious material.

2

TOKUJIN YOSHIOKA
Tokujin Yoshioka

2009
1 Cloud Sofa and Armchair
Producer: Moroso

1

RICHARD HUTTEN

2004-2008
2 Muybridge Chair
Material: Lasercut MDF
Producer: Richard Hutten Studio

Muybridge is named after the homonymous pioneer of photography Eadweard Muybridge. Hutten, a photographer himself, took a series of pictures of himself in profile while rising from a seated position, capturing this single movement in 53 images, according to the same system that made Muybridge famous. The pictures were enlarged, laser-cut in MDF slices and glued together in the order in which they were taken. The resulting seat literally allows users to sit in the designer's lap while the movement of his rising figure provides an armrest. "Time has been transformed into furniture," says Hutten.

2

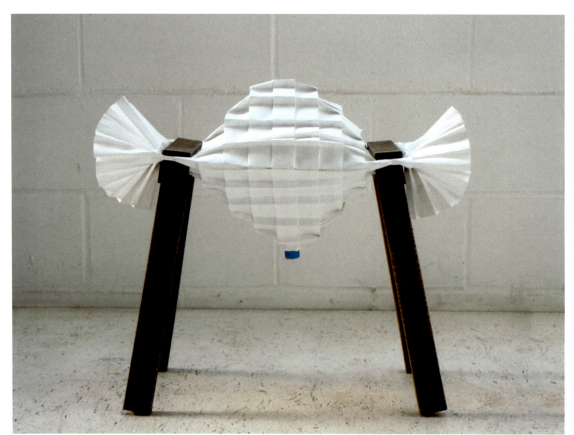

RAW-EDGES
Yael Mer & Shay Alkalay

2009
Pleated Pleat Seating
Material: DuPont™ Tyvek®,
polyurethane foam
Photography: Shay Alkalay
Producer: Craft Punk / Design Miami, Fendi

Borrowing a technique used in fashion production, the designers folded and re-folded DuPont™ Tyvek® to create a series of plush seats. The method of pleating allows the flat, non-elastic material to become a springy, three-dimensional cushion when filled with soft polyurethane foam.

FULGURO
Yves Fidalgo & Cédric Decroux

2009
1 Les Liseuses
Photography: Fulguro

LAURENT MASSALOUX

2009
2 Curiosité
Material: Black translucent resin, laser
sintering system, feathers
Producer: Tools Galerie
Photography: Laurent Massaloux

PUNGA AND SMITH

2009
3 Beast Rug
Material: Wool felt and brass
Photography: Punga & Smith

Constructed from wool felt with a folded
sheet brass skull the *Beast Rug* is a whimsi-
cal alternative to a classic bear skin rug.

1

2

3

Fluxus Furniture

1

2

3

4

5

6

1

3

5

JOHANNES HEMANN

2008
1 **Geoffrey Armchair**
Material: Foam
Photography: Lena Billo

2008
2 **Irmela Pendant Lamp**
Material: Polypropylen

2008
3 **Emma Pendant Lamp**
Material: Styrofoam, varnish
Photography: Lena Billo

Lighting based on forms generated by storms; not the destructive force of wind, but energy-generating forces, as seen in sand dunes and snow drifts.

2008
4 **Oswine Pendant Lamp**
Material: Polypropylene
Photography: Lena Billo

2008
5 **Paula Pendant Lamp**
Material: Plexiglas
Photography: Lena Billo

2008
6 **Kirsten Pendant Lamp**
Material: Polypropylene

6

2008
Clutch Chair
Material: Candy-stripe drinking straws
Photography: Scott Jarvie

Made from 10,000 drinking straws, the *Clutch Chair* is an experimental piece that passes judgement on our disposable culture. The piece was developed through observation of the structural characteristics of trees and selected by Zaha Hadid as her Curator's Choice at Noise Festival 2008.

1

2

3

4

SCRAP LAB

2008
1 Black Spider Chair
Material: Steel, discarded plastic strips
Photography: Florian Gypser
Producer: scraplab

2008
2 Silicone Chair
Material: Steel, modified silicone tubes
Photography: Florian Gypser
Producer: scraplab

2008
3 Denim Chair
Material: Steel, scrap denim
Photography: Florian Gypser
Producer: scraplab

BOOKHOU
John Booth

2006
4 Chair
Material: Recycled furniture parts,
maple wood
Photography: bookhou
Producer: bookhou

1

ARIHIRO MIYAKE

2009
1 **FORT Partition System**
Material: Polyester Fibre, NdFeB Magnet,
Styrene Foam
Photography: Chikako Harada
Producer: Prototype

An acoustic partition system, formed out
of recycled PET bottle fiber. The assembly
is by the integrated magnets allowing easy
modification and unlimited extendability of
the system.

KRÄUTLI

Florian Kräutli

2008
2 **Magnetic Curtain**
Material: Fabric, Magnets
Photography: Florian Kräutli
Producer: Droog Design

A curtain that can assume any form via
magnets integrated into its fabric.

2

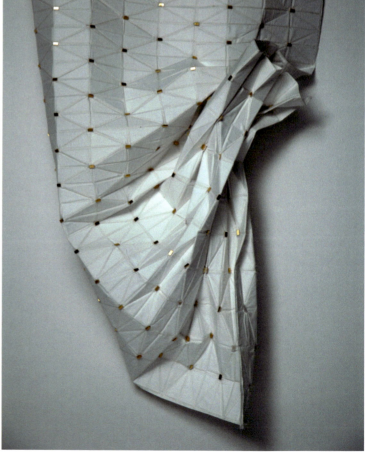

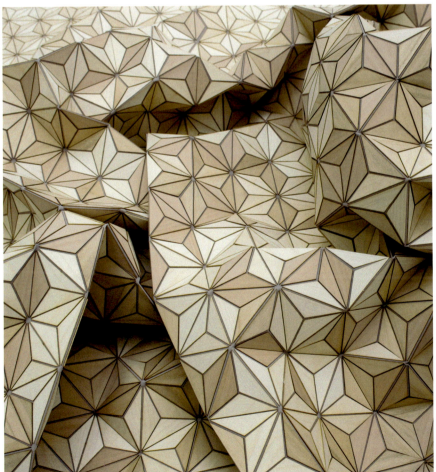

ELISA STROZYK

2009
Wooden Carpet
Material: Wood veneer and textile
Photography: Sebastian Neeb
Producer: Elisa Strozyk

The *Wooden Carpet* forms part of the collection *Wooden Textiles* which experiments with wood in new ways. Geometric wooden *paillettes* form a flexible surface, much like sequins, with the ability to function in different three-dimensional shapes. The material blurs hard and soft, parquet and carpet, furniture and textile. A wooden textile can become a blanket, rug, shelter or tablecloth.

A Tale Told by Design

In the age of postmodernism – and given that classic modernism is enjoying a renaissance – ____

____ it would seem opportune to ask whether there might also be some relevant point within pre-modernism that would be suitable for shaping the perception of design in the 21st century.

If design still wishes to pursue an ethical approach, the ideas of modernism are perhaps far less appropriate to serve as moral guidelines in the present day than we generally assume. Modernism developed its ethical concept for an emergent industrial society and demanded

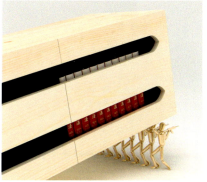

Daniel Loves Objects (2009)

– in the best, well-intentioned sense – an industrialisation of all areas of life. This alone promised a broad strata of the population a share in the material resources and the satisfaction of their basic human needs. Shortage of materials and rationalised production methods were supposed to yield cheap products that wanted to be nothing more in appearance than what was obvious from their technical function. The radicalism of this aesthetic drew its power from the exclusion of any decorative elements, the absolute renunciation of artisan (i.e. individual) interpretations of a design, and a doctrine of simplicity in the choice of materials. One famous photo series dating from 1928 – the year in which Marcel Breuer developed his Wassily Chair – portrays the successful dramatist Bertolt Brecht smoking a cigar and wrapped in a leather jacket. Brecht flirted with the regalia of bourgeois and proletarian power simultaneously, thereby shocking a bourgeois society that was already starting to unravel. We can only imagine what kind of impact leather must have had as the seat material on the Bauhaus cantilever chair when it had previously been confined to the coachman's footstool. One thing was certain: the bourgeoisie sat on fabric.

Folklore

When modernism took root in industrial design, the last artistic reform movement to be infused with the handcraft ideal – Art Nouveau – had been dead for just fifteen years and the British Arts and Crafts Movement for just thirty. But within less than half a century, the context of social and technological development had undergone such radical change that the principles of these movements now looked distinctly outmoded. Today there is a strong suspicion that the design of classic modernism could meet with a similar fate because the social and technological development of the past decades has created a different context. We live in postmodernism, which in this case is not taken to mean the aesthetically-defined period but rather the richly diverse possibilities for experiencing our society and its manifestations following the demise of modernism's defining context: industrial society.

As with historism in the Victorian age, life as a postmodernist designer makes it possible to browse the stylistic diversity of the pre-modern era and borrow from it. But because we (at least in the West) have long since departed from the context of industrial production, it is also possible – in contrast to historism – for us to borrow from pre-industrial manufacturing techniques. This is where a genuine renaissance of handcraft comes into play. Because if we use the admittedly rather German definition of the design concept for

Snodevormgevers (2008)

industrial production, what we are currently experiencing is not a paradigm shift in design but the unbelievable revival of a discipline whose powers of innovation had been pronounced virtually dead. It is no coincidence that the meaning of handcraft has now regained such strength that parallels can be drawn with the 19th century – i.e. with pre-modern times. Given the already largely industrialised nature of construction activity by the middle of that century, the German architect Gottfried Semper saw handcraft as the only creative force with the potential to bring about a new artistic beginning in architecture –

something the avant-garde believed was urgently necessary. The Arts and Crafts Movement that began at the same time in Britain saw handcraft as the only discipline capable of creating an authentic style for the 19th century. Arts and Crafts emerged in response to the historism of the Victorian era and the perception that the objects of in-

PatriciaUrquiola (2009)

dustrial production in those years were largely soulless. This was because the design-determining style of production – historism – only borrowed ornamental ideas from art history that could be manufactured by machines. The focus was not on formal aesthetic considerations but on deciding which ornaments could most easily be copied using the possibilities of industrial machinery. It is hardly surprising, then, that the protagonists of the Arts and Crafts Movement regarded machines as the root of all evil. As a counterweight to what they saw as soulless machine production, they believed in a return to the qualities and techniques of handcraft. And in order to cast this handcraft in an especially radiant light, their own designs displayed a rustic, even folkloristic language of form and decoration. But the only thing they had in common with genuine folk art was the content of their imagery. In formal terms, their work amounted to a new and independent interpretation. This is the exact point at which the current trend towards folklore in design sets to work. Once again the aim is to materialise a vision of ideal life – not

as before in opposition to the threatening ills of the industrial age, but as an antipode to the increasing digitalisation in all fields of our lives.

Roustique references

It is therefore no surprise that the protagonists of the current handcraft renaissance look to the folk art of past epochs as a source from which to borrow. The central attributes of the Arts and Crafts Movement – simplicity and a serious treatment of the material – which at that time were best expressed by folkloristic art, can also be applied to current thinking. In contemporary design, the notion of the authentic plays an equally important role as it did then, with the difference that the result – an authentic product – can be achieved in postmodernism via an array of parallel design approaches. Digging around in the dusty catacombs of pre-modern folk art is just one possibility for lending objects a certain authenticity. Admittedly it is an extremely tempting one, considering that it forms an obvious antithesis to the still prevalent belief that an authentic product must imitate the radical simplicity of classic modernism. This new Arts and Crafts Movement gains its appeal from the physically tangible process of making things, the independent creation of objects – in contrast to the task of

Reddish Studio (2007)

designing for industrial production. Particularly from the ethical perspective of design, this new Arts and Crafts Movement is exploring unchartered territory. And nobody can seriously refute its argument.

Alchemy experience

It shows that authenticity can also look refreshingly different. Through the interplay of intensive materiality, handcrafted decorative elements and rustic forms, for example, objects are produced with a dramatic edge that has not previously been seen. Their narrative qualities offer powerful resistance to the inexpressive mass-produced wares of our thoroughly demystified world. And so in a remarkable way, new magic is breathed into the profane everyday object. Whereby the initial approach of the designers is not entirely unlike that of the much-maligned historism. References from different epochs are blended together in a highly non-dogmatic manner. But in the handcraft process, a form is created that manages to absorb and assimilate that break in aesthetics like a virtual time machine. It is the creative process of handcraft that knows how to infuse objects with feelings and associations from different epochs, without the overall appearance of the object suffering. On the contrary: each detail provides meaning while the whole magically assumes a sense of history. And it offers the user an opportunity to regard the objects as authentic and therefore meaningful.

Dustdeluxe (2009)

Luxury in craft / gracious living

This new definition of the authentic object opens up a broad spectrum of possibilities for design. Liberated from the dictates of industrial production conditions, we can see a new object universe emerging that appears unfettered by limitations. While its thematic inspiration may be taken from the epochs of art history, it still succeeds in developing an original quality – in contrast to historism. The important point for the designers is to make the individual creative act visible. And indeed, the time that was invested in producing an object is there to be seen. It is the personal, valuable labour of the craftsman that makes an object so impressive for its user and observer – and moves us to acknowledge its monetary value more quickly than if it were a machine-produced object. Through the craftsman's interpretation, the apparently inauthentic is made real by his/her skill in the production process. Challenging details – such as the joining of shaped components or different materials – attain the power of naturalness. The result is a new luxury which – rather than being ostentatious – is rooted in the cultural history of handcraft design.

Studio Job (2008)

STUDIO JOB
Job Smeets + Nynke Tynagel

2009
1 The Birth of The Gospel
Material: Polychrome handblown glass,
lead, Indian rosewood
Photography: R. Kot, Brussels
Producer: Studio Job/ ING art collection
Collection Zuiderzee Museum

STUDIO JOB
Job Smeets + Nynke Tynagel

2009
**The Last Supper and The Crucifixion
of The Gospel**
Material: Corroded foundry iron, candle,
polychrome handblown glass, lead,
Indian rosewood
Photography: R. Kot, Brussels
Producer: Studio Job/ ING art collection
Collection Zuiderzee Museum

Job Smeets + Nynke Tynagel

2008
1 **Bavaria Cabinet**
2 **Bavaria Screen**
3 **Bavaria Bench**
4 **Bavaria Table**
  Material: Indian rosewood, polychrome
  dyed through veneers in 17 colours, multiply wood, brass
  Photography: R. Kot, Brussels
  Producer: Studio Job
  Courtesy Moss, NY

1

2

3

4

Although architect and industrial designer Patricia Urquiola digs deep into her Spanish roots for inspiration, she has earned – through her choice of collaborations and her location – an honoured position in the Italian design pantheon. Urquiola knew that she wanted to be an architect by the time she was twelve. Today, her eclectic design process has produced a consistently original body of work that is just as refreshingly diverse.

In general, Urquiola has a talent for combining unconventional forms with unexpected textures and layered patterns or colours to produce highly graphical furniture. Her *Crinoline* outdoor fan chair for B&B exaggerates the traditional throne-like backrest of the type while embedding large floral patterns into what looks like standard wicker weave (which is actually made from polyethylene). For the Italian brand Emu, her loopy, brightly coloured, line of outdoor furniture called *RE-TROUVÉ* is both inspired yet circumvents the conventionality of iron garden chairs popular during the 1950s. More austere but equally shapely, is Urquiola's *Pear* bath furniture for Agape. (She has also ventured into the bathroom – with an all-white palette – for Axor, as well.)

Like a novelist who fictionalizes real life, Urquiola often looks to craft techniques, human behaviour and (often Spanish) historical and cultural memory for ideas that she then translates and updates in her own peculiar manner. The designer's eight-carpet series for GAN (Gandia Blasco's carpet and textile label) is called *Mangas*, or "sleeves." These carpets take their visual cues from the shapes of traditional Spanish shirt-sleeves, from the *manga corta* (short sleeve) to the *manga da campana* (bell sleeve), and create a patchwork of multi-scale knitted floor-coverings in unusual shapes. A fine example of Urquiola's dexterity in translating ordinary regional cultural habits into contemporary products, *Mangas* maintain an unassailable aesthetic integrity and communicate an immediate modernity despite their eclectic textures, knit scales and colours. Urquiola accomplished this, as well, with a series of rugs for Moroso. For them, she modernized traditional Sardinian animal and plant motifs by playing with scale, colour, and collaged, off-centre composition.

Urquiola has a pedigree equal to her talent. Born in 1961 in Oviedo, in northern Spain, Urquiola studied architecture at the Faculdad de Arquitectura de Madrid, transferring to, and then graduating from Milan's Polytechnic in 1989 where her thesis advisor was architect Achille Castiglioni. By 1991, she began to design for and to direct product development at the furniture company De Padova in Milan, working frequently with Vico Magistretti. From 1993 to 1996 she designed architecture and interiors for showrooms and restaurants in a practice shared with two friends before she began to manage the Lissoni Associati Design Group. She was designing under her own name, simultaneously, however, for Kartell, Molteni & C., Knoll and Moroso, and would finally open her own Milan-based practice five years later.

It is Urquiola's collaborations with Patrizia Moroso, which began in 1998, that have lent the greatest flavour to her body of work and allowed the designer to show her legend-making range of expression. Entirely remaking the Arne Jacobsen *Egg* chair to which it pays homage, Urquiola's *Fjord* chaise celebrates an unusual asymmetry. Her *Tropicalia* chairs consist of joyously clashing colours – dark purple, petal pink, emerald, sky blue, lemon yellow – rendered in translucent thermoplastic polymer threads, polyester cords and (more refined and sober) leather bands woven onto tubular steel frames. Through her work, Urquiola honours contradictions, progress and resourcefulness – the human condition, in a nutshell.

www.patriciaurquiola.com

PATRICIA URQUIOLA

2009
Mangas
Producer: Gandia Blasco

1

FORMAFANTASMA
Andrea Trimarchi & Simone Farresin

2008
1 Set in Concrete Sculptural Object
   Material: Concrete, porcelain
   Photography: Formafantasma
   Producer: Formafantasma

We have grown accustomed to perceiving objects as invisible presences without history or substance. Everything is designed to be easily absorbed into our lives and just as easily disposed of. In this context, lightness seems to be the only value that remains. In protest, the designers created "an ode to heaviness," that gives metaphorical and literal weight the ordinary things that surround us and then elevates the objects by placing them on a stone pedestal. As iconic materials, stone, marble and concrete communicate both heaviness and immortalilty, honoring the value of simple objects. The logo on the plinth refers to and highlights the handmaking of the pieces.

2009
2 Hidden Clock
   Material: OSB, resin, veneer
   Photography: Formafantasma
   Producer: Formafantasma

Instead of focusing on the design of a clock, Formafantasma focused instead on its packaging. On a conceptual level, packaging represents the imago of the object. Starting with a cheap catalog-bought clock, the designers strove to move packaging from the level of image to substance. *Hidden Clock* represents the multiple boxes that swaddle an objcet from factory to shop and which fetishize the packaging itself since making the container more valuable than the contents requires box upon box to protect the one beneath it.

2009
2 Hidden Tools
   Material: OSB, resin, veneer
   Photography: Formafantasma
   Producer: Formafantasma

The inlaid décor of a box at the table's center stands in contrast to the industrial assemblage of inexpensive OSB in which it is embedded. The designers integrated inlays – in the shape of the tools used to fashion the table – into the chipboard and then refined it with a layer of clear resin. Elevated from worthless to precious via this superficial coating, the nature of the object is nonetheless revealed when the box is opened and found to contain only sawdust.

2

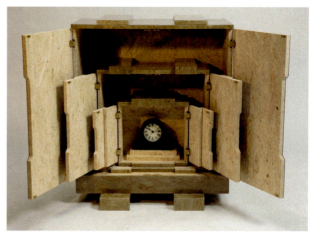

3

FREDRIK FÄRG

2009
Modus:cover Cupboard
Material: Stained oak, MDF, stained and
varnished PLAZA magazine pages
Producer:MöbelsnickarmästareJohansson

Modus:cover is a cupboard dressed in the
fashions of the day it was built. Färg sheathed
it in style magazines and then stained and
varnished the exterior to obscure their
pages. The inspiration for this piece came
in part from that magical moment when,
while renovating a house, one discovers
newspapers, as old as the house, beneath the
wallpaper, revealing and reifying the historical context of the building. The use of the
fashion magazine was intended to serve as
a record of time and place and to point out,
as Färg suggests, that the charm of manufactured objects often tends to obscure their
historical value.

1

2

TORD BOONTJE

2009
1 Flower Table
Producer: Moroso

MAARTEN KOLK & GUUS KUSTERS
Maarten Kolk

2006
2 Herbaria
Material: Pressed/dried vegetables,
textiles, wood
Photography: Maarten Kolk

Giving new meaning to the term "preserves,"
Herbaria was Kolk's exercise in observing
the limits of natural plant growth.

MARTIN BERGSTRÖM

2009
3 UFOMYRAN
Material: Upholstery Fabric
Producer: Carl Malmsten

Bergstöm found his inspiration under-
ground, among a tree's roots. There will be a
limited edition of 10 unique armchairs covered in this fabric for Malmstenbutiken.

3

2008

1 **Hidden Layers:**
  Peeling Wallpaper Cupboard
2 **Hidden Layers:**
  Peeling Wallpaper Sideboard
  Material: Screenprinted MDF
  Photography: Emma Nilsson

Could wear and tear on furniture be decorative? No doubt, in Folkform's estimation. The collection *Hidden Layers* comprises a number of cabinets in which experiments were carried out using various surfaces and materials, to re-create cracks and natural wear.

2008

3 **Light Box Lamps and Partition**
  Material: Wood, polyester resin
  Photography: Kaman Tung
  Producer: Studio Jo Meesters

Light Box is a series of lamps created in the tradition of cabinetmaking. The wooden lamp features a pattern of 8.000 perforations reinforced with transparent resin. In combination with the illustration of low-lying trees, *Light Box* is also a room divider in the shape of an artificial hedge or a nocturnal, domestic landscape.

1

2

3

1

REDDISH STUDIO
Naama Steinbock & Idan Friedman

2007
1 Yakuza Table
Material: Veneered MDF
Photography: Dan Lev
Producer: Reddish Studio

A table treated as a living body, and digitally tattooed, receiving its character from the pattern printed on its surface. The wood texture acts as skin, becoming a platform for expressing a cultural and personal identity. The digital printing technology enabled Reddish to treat each table individually, making them unique.

JUDITH SENG

2008
2 Patches Lowboard
Material: Coated wood, veneer (maple, poplar, red oak, bog oak, cherry)
Photography: Gallery Post Design, Carlo Ninchi
Producer: Memphis s.r.l.

2

SNODEVORMGEVERS
Mander Liefting & Josef Blersch

2008
1 Fireplace / Tree Trunk Series
2 Liquor Cabinet / Tree Trunk Series
3 Fireplace / Tree Trunk Series
4 Gentleman's Chamber 1953, aka
   Tree Trunk Series
   Material: Steelplate, polyurethane coating
   Photography: Josef Blersch
   Producer: Snodevormgevers

Gentleman's Chamber 1953 is a fusion of outdoors and interior: Traditional elements from a gentleman's bedroom are reinterpreted from the point of view of animals. The fireplace , the liquor cabinet and the stools are made from tree trunks, or so it appears. On closer inspection users will notice that they are actually made from steel plate.

1

2

3

4

POUR LES ALPES
Annina Gähwiler & Tina Stieger

2008
Echos Collection
Material: Swiss pine, spruce, 2-K multiply coated ebony, chestnut, fiberglass, epoxy resin coating, lace, silk and cotton
Photography: Till Forrer
Producer: Pour les Alpes

This furniture collection is made up of three chests of drawers that have been created in collaboration with five artisan craftsmen from two Swiss regions, Grisons and Appenzell. Shingle-making, wood-carving and lace-making techniques are living crafts in the Swiss alpine region and deeply rooted in everyday life. The individual objects are a tribute to the Swiss Alps and, in a formal and symbolic way, refer to the local alpine identity and culture. Each piece awakens memories while offering room for interpretation. The names of the pieces – *Ehrfurcht* (Reverence), *Neugierde* (Curiosity) and *Sehnsucht* (Desire) – describe a personal and regional perspective.

Roustique Reference

2008
1 **Patchwork Cabinet 01**
2 **Patchwork Cabinet 02**
   Material: Oak, ceramics, bronze, glass
   Photography: Frank Tielemans

1

2

ALEX HELLUM

2008
1 Heals Discovers Dressing Table

The designer decided to make a dressing table without a drawer, replacing the drawer with a ring tree and mirror, both mounted in a wooden dish. For additional storage, a felt pouch hangs under the table for jewelry and smaller items.

2009
2 Furniture in a Box Stool
  Material: Ash
  Photography: Ulrik Stool (SCP)
  Producer: SCP

Hellum plays on traditional design and craft values by using the vernacular language of traditional furniture.

2007
3 Heals Discovers Hall/Bedroom Chair
  Material: Beech, felt
  Producer: Ercol

A piece that combines coat rack with a surface on which to sit and tie your shoelaces.

1

2

3

Roustique Reference

BO REUDLER

2009
Slow White Series:
Slow White Cabinet, Slow White Chair,
Slow White Table and Golden Compass
Material: Found wood (beech, birch, cherry or oak), recy-
cled timber, white linseed-oil paint, metal coating.
Photography: Bo Reudler Studio
Producer: Bo Reudler Studio

We tend to present nature in a controlled way: branches sim-
plified into repetitive patterns, majestic trees trimmed into
squared beams, flowers flattened into graphic motifs. In this
way, nature's complexity, randomness and rawness is tamed.
Reudler believes that people have lost their connection to
nature and even our immediate surroundings and that this
century will be a time to renew this connection. For *Slow
White*, he gathered fallen wood and transformed it by hand
into furniture. He selected branches for their distinguishing
imperfections and curves. Following their shapes led him to
the final forms: the individual branches were numbered and
the pieces are composed using a carefully considered combination of them.

Through everyday objects, furniture and interiors, Marcel Wanders manufactures fragments of dreams. The Dutch director of Marcel Wanders Studio, and art director and co-founder of mass-market design label Moooi, envisions life as a fairytale in which the handmade is mass-produced and, at any moment, rooms sprout into enchanted forests. "I'm very enthusiastic about and dedicated to decorative, and warm and detailed surroundings. But then I also design very 'skinny' products," Wanders says. "I don't do superficial decorative things. And I wouldn't call them minimal. I would call them optimal."

Venus Chair (2009)

Indeed, Wanders' use of ornament can be exuberant. Usually, however, his lush syntheses of patterns are lain over the most austere forms, so that curlicues and flourishes are engaging without becoming overwhelming. He also strategically combines the industrial with the handmade and the old with the new, with the understanding that form no longer needs to remain shackled to function. And then, he employs decoration to make the product reach beyond simple operational proficiency to tell a story, elicit a feeling, fascinate through fantasy.

Wanders was sent down from the Design Academy of Eindhoven after only one year, but redoubled his academic efforts at a craft and jewellery school in Maastricht and ended by graduating with honours from the Arnhem School of the Arts in 1988. Five years later, Wanders joined Gijs Bakker and Remy Rammakers at Droog Design's first Milan exhibition. It was for Droog that he produced his now-iconic *Knotted Chair* in 1996. From 1995, the designer worked under the name Wanders Wonders, until 2001 when he established the Marcel Wanders Studio in Amsterdam and, with Casper Vissers, co-founded Moooi. Now, he is installed on the crowning floors of a former schoolhouse in the centre of the city where the walls and floors are sheathed in his relentlessly crowded and colourful designs.

Though most people see only his products, his larger projects, including residential, hotel and restaurant interiors, are actually rich accretions and evolutions of the furniture and product. It is Wanders' talent for scenography and theatre that lend the larger "stagings" coherence. His stagecraft is also evident when Wanders "designs" events that seem to play out somewhere between dream and reality: in 2008, Wanders staged *Aqua Jewels* to introduce his Swarovski Shandelier: Bikini-clad models bathed in the light and water flowed from three ornate chandeliers that were actually showerheads. Guests visiting his Mondrian Hotel in Miami, the opulence of which was inspired by Sleeping Beauty's castle (easily evoked by Wanders' custom furniture), may have the sensation of awaking after a prolonged, and rather dull, sleep. And for those who have suspected all along that life is, indeed, a dream, Wanders ensures that it's a good one.

www.marcelwanders.com

2009
Parent Chair and Table
Photography: Mooi
Producer: Moooi

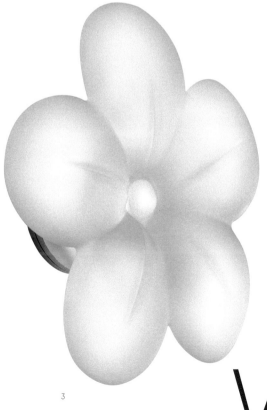

2009
1 Can Can Light
Producer: Flos

2007
2 Skygarden Light
Producer: Flos

2009
3 Wallflower
Producer: Flos

MARCEL
WANDERS

Roustique Reference
159

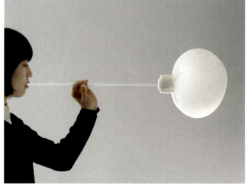

NENDO
Oki Sato

2009
Blown-Fabric Lamp
Material: Unwoven fabric
Photography: Masayuki Hayashi

Nendo created *Blown-Fabric* for Tokyo Fiber'09 Senseware, an exhibition intended to convey the possibilities of new materials developed with Japanese synthetic fibre technology. *Smash* is a long-fibre nonwoven polyester that can be manipulated into different forms through hot press forming technology. Because it is thermoplastic, lightweight and rip-proof, but glows beautifully when light passes through it, designer Oki Sato used it to create lighting fixtures in the style of vernacular Japanese *chochin* paper lanterns. The structure of standard *chochin* consists of thin strips of bamboo wrapped around a wood frame, reinforced with vertical stitching and then pasted with Japanese mulberry paper which gives them their characteristic glow. *Smash*'s properties allowed Nendo to form it like blown glass into a seamless one-piece lantern. Because it is impossible to entirely control the process, each fixture takes a unique form as heat is added and pressurized air blown into it. As in glass-blowing, the maker can influence the production of each piece, resulting in a collection of objects whose infinitely varied imperfections are reminiscent of the infinite formal mutations of viruses and bacteria in response to environmental changes, and a far cry from the standardized forms of industrial mass-production.

1

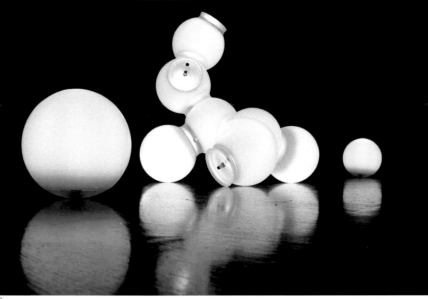

2

KENSAKU OSHIRO

2009
1 Silk Ball Lantern
Material: Silk, aluminium
Photography: Beppe Brancato

To create *Silk Ball*, Oshiro drew on a special
silk thread extraction technology which was
originally developed for the production of
Japanese kimonos.

MAARTEN DE CEULAER

2008
2 Nomad Light Molecule
Material: PE, PMMA, LEDs

PIERRE KRACHT

2007
1 Käte Pendant Light
Material: Cable
Photograph: Ebbo Rothe
Producer: Pierre Kracht

Function follows form, form follows function.
Knitted from 50 meters cable and lit with
one lightbulb, *Käte* becomes a symbol of our
times: hand-craft meets technology, something both complex and yet understandable.

HUMANS SINCE 1982
Per Emanuelsson & Bastian Bischoff

2007
2 Celebrating the Cross 1 Chaise Longue
Material: Wood, metal

1

2

BRIKOLÖR

2009
Pärlan Chair
Material: Wood, laminated wood, solid ash
Photography: Niclas Löfgren
Producer: Brikolör

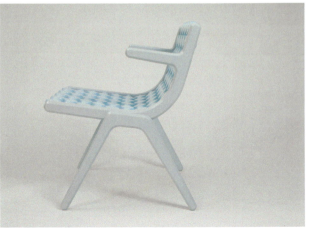

IMAGINARY OFFICE
Daniel Hedner

2009
1 Pleats-Pleats Sofa
Material: Tubular steel, polyurethane
foam, jersey textile
Photograph: Karl Sandoval

The *Pleats-Pleats* sofa is made by welding
and weaving together steel, polyurethane
and textile. This unconventional weave
comes from the hybrid idea of a blown-up
knit and a large-scale seating "landscape"
and suggests an *Alice in Wonderland* theme.
Pleats consists of 19, 3.5-meter long cords
which are individually sheathed in yellow
jersey fabric before being woven together
using a macramé technique.

KWANGHO LEE

2009
2 Obsession Sofa
Material: Gardening Hoses
Photograph: Kwangho Lee

1

2

BYAMT INC
Alissia Melka-Teichroew

2008
1 **Chair Mix A Lot**
2 **Grandfather Clock Wall Stickers**
   Material: Vinyl Wall Stickers
   Photography: Blik Surface Graphics
   Producer: Blik Surface Graphics

Add an element of drama to your home with the Silhouette Set! Inspired by theater design and Kinder egg surprises, byAMT has created a kit of furniture stickers that are life-sized but rendered as two-dimensional silhouettes: a dresser, grandfather clock, two chairs and some accessories.

CLAUDIO COLUCCI DESIGN

2008
3 **Mutant Series Bench**
   Photography: Takumi Ota / Clear Gallery
   Producer: Clear Gallery, Japan

3

1

2

ALAIN GILLES

2009
1 **Big Table**
Photography: Bonaldo
Producer: Bonaldo

FORMFORYOU

2008
2 **Peg Collection Lighting**
(WallPeg, WindowPeg and FloorPeg)
Material: Metal sheet
Photography: Pelle Wahlgren
Producer: Bsweden belysningsbolaget

From the ordinary peg, formforyou have
created a lighting series.

Alchemy Experience
167

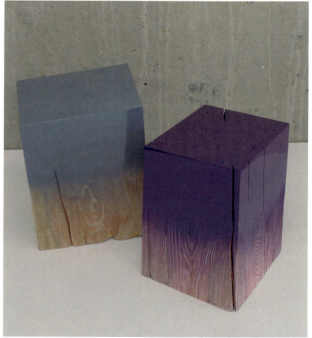

BRIKOLÖR

2009
1 **Lodlärk Cabinet**
2 **Våglärk Console**
   Material: Wood, solid larch
   Photography: Niclas Löfgren

JUDITH SENG

2009
3 **TRIFT Stool**
   Material: Lacquered solid wood
   Photography: Judith Seng

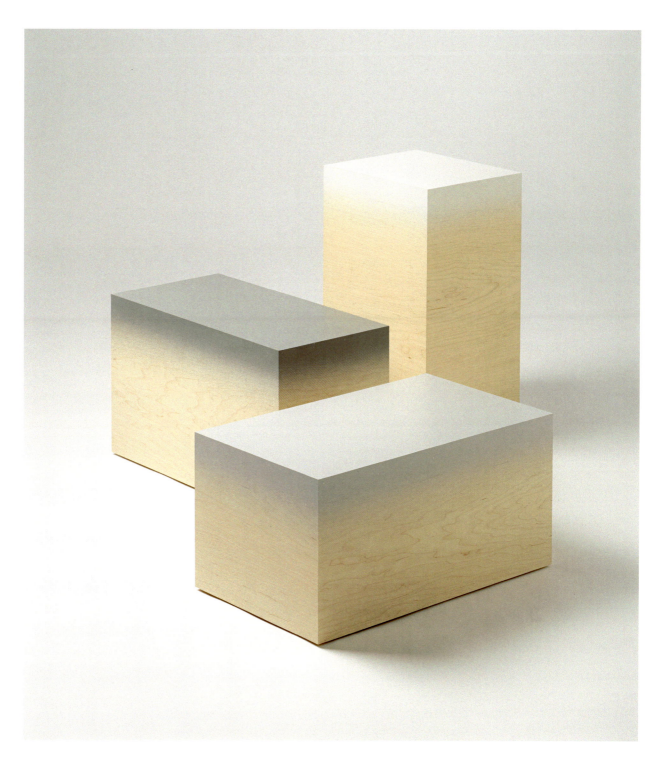

BIG-GAME
Grégoire Jeanmonod, Elric Petit and
Augustin Scott de Martinville

200099
BLUR Tables
Material: Maple silkscreened with a
watermarked gradient
Photography: Michel Bonvin
Producer: Big-Game

1

DUSTDELUXE
Damien Gernay

2009
1 Textured Sideboard
Material: MDF, polyurethane, fake wood
Photography: Tine Claerhout
Producer: DUSTDELUXE

GOLRAN

2 Carpet Reloaded

Golran patches together old carpets to create its one-off and limited-edition custom line. The seamed rugs have been decolorized and re-dyed, unthreaded, cut-up, re-woven and sewn back together again by artisanal weavers working with cotton, wool, angora, black goat's wool, hemp, mohair and linen.

2

REDDISH STUDIO

2008
1 Sucker
Material: Wood, steel
Photography: Dan Lev
Producer: Reddish studio

A gradient cabinet. *Sucker* incorporates two approaches to furniture design. Instead of choosing between the two, the furniture appearance changes from a bare natural material to a synthetic unifying colour.

JUDITH SENG

2008
2 RISE Series
Material: Wood, coated, brushed and treated with acid
Photography: Gallery Post Design/ Carlo Ninchi
Producer: Memphis s.r.l.

RISE confronts the manufacturing of perfect surfaces by creating and destroying them in the same object. The cultural consensus that we must strive for perfection is challenged by an emerging aesthetic that is based in the nihilistic interventions of nature and man. *RISE* meditates on this ambivalence and is presented as a reflection on current aesthetics.

2

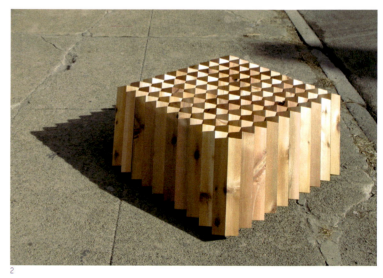

PEPE HEYKOOP

2009
1 **Soft Oak Chair**
Material: Oak, foam
Photography: Pepe Heykoop
Producer: Studio Pepe Heykoop

Heykoop's chair is about the contrast of its framework. It keeps a little secret in its seat. To minimize the use of fabric he applied a mosaic of oak "tiles" to the cushions.

TAKESHI MIYAKAWA DESIGN

2009
2 **Axonometric 2 Bench**
Material: Cedar
Photography: Takeshi Miyakawa

A sculptural investigation of the "axonometric" drawing of a cube. By staggering rhombic extrusions in a grid, a perfectly square top and cross-section is created.

KHAI LIEW

2007
3 **Dancing Girls Cabinet**
4 **Minton Cabinet**
Material: Solid English limewood
Photography: Grant Hancock
Producer: Khai Liew Design

3

4

JULIAN MAYOR

2008
1 Angle Chair
Material: Cardboard
Producer: Julian Mayor

BRIKOLÖR

2009
2 Hägg Cabinet
Material: Ash veneer
Pattern by Rasmus Hägg
Photography: Johanna Ekmark

EMMEMOBILI

3 Stripes
Producer: Emmemobili

1

3

1

RYAN DART DESIGN

2009
1 Quarry Bench
Material: Plywood
Photography: ryandartdesign

TINA ROEDER

Tina Roeder & David Krings

2008
2 Structures / Facades Credenza
Material: Cardboard, chrome-plated steel
Photography: Guido Mieth

A credenza or sideboard prototype inspired by the architecture of East and West Berlin, like the famous socialist ensemble on Karl-Marx-Allee or the Hansaviertel in the former West: visionary and rich in utopias.

2

"I like marrying opposites because they enrich each other," says Berlin-based Dutch product designer Hella Jongerius. "I also like the marriage between industry and craft, which is a great way of innovating." Indeed, she reconciles seeming contradictions in the form of techniques, materials and concept. Not only has the small team at Jongeriuslab mixed glass and ceramics in her familiar *Long Neck* and *Groove Bottles*, and embroidery thread with porcelain to sew her new-fangled Delftware, it has also long chosen to bounce between high design and widely affordable pieces, working for Vitra and Paris' Galerie Kreo as often as IKEA. The designer and Eindhoven Academy professor produced her limited-edition Natura Design Magistra for Kreo at the same time that she developed a trio of wall-hangings for IKEA and Unicef. The Kreo project comprised a simple wooden table with a sculpture of an oversized frog climbing from one leg onto the tabletop, along with fabric vases filled with fake flowers.

#1 Artificial Pink Vase (2009)

Also for Kreo, Jongerius designed the Swatch table series, which visualizes her belief that design should offers options instead of so-called Truths. On close examination, each coloured cast-polyurethane "tile" in the tabletop is actually made up of multiple colours, even though it appears from a distance to represent only one. Embedded, flush in an irregularly angular walnut "setting," like jewels in a piece of jewellery, the depth and translucence of the material lend a sense of layering to a structurally straightforward object.

Jongerius has long layered narrative into her products either through literal strata of textile, as with her *Pelle*, *Mikkel* and *Gullspira* felted wool hangings for Ikea, which were based on a goat, fox and rabbit from Swedish fairytales and hand-stitched by Indian seamstresses, or by letting latent imagination burst out of the product, as with her frog table, also for Kreo. This kind of work was first introduced with the one-off *Props* series – snail-vases, feathered pitchers, dragonfly-ladles – that Jongerius produced for a Vitra booth at the Milan furniture fair. Again, the designer envisioned hybrids between functional products and fabled characters, underscoring the contemporary meaning of "functionality" in design, which encompasses not just operational "function" and simple utility, but which takes on a broader storytelling, emotion-eliciting (and often thereby, branding) function. This was further developed in hybrid mythical-beast-cum-task-furniture designed for Vitra and titled *Office Pets*.

What is the value of each kind of design – the limited-edition gallery objects and the commercially accessible products – to Jongerius? The projects for clients like Kreo let her experiment and be innovative – to "fill her library" for use during more industrial projects; on the other hand, work for clients like Ikea presents a new challenge because everyone must be able to afford it: "To make work for Ikea customers, you have to design for the mainstream. To buy it, many people have to think the product is good, because they will not buy it just because of my name," she says. "It's more difficult to go beyond your own taste than to be expressive." How does she design with that breadth then? "I have a few people in my mind who have to like it even though they will never actually see it," Jongerius smiles, "My mother, my sister-in-law, my neighbours."

www.jongeriuslab.com

2009
Artificial Vases Set – Collection natura design magistra
Material: Glass, blownglass, ceramic, plastic, leather, wood
Photography: Fabrice Gousset
Producer: Galerie kreo

HELLA JONGERIUS

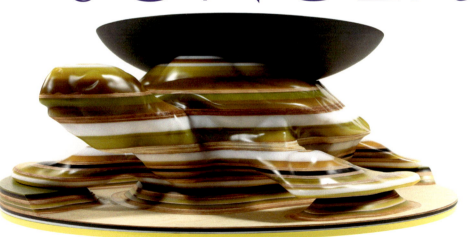

2009

1 **Frog Table – Collection Natura Design Magistra**
Material: French walnut wood and blue transparent enamel
Photography: ©Fabrice Gousset
Producer: Galerie kreo

2 **Turtle Coffee Table – Collection Natura Design Magistra**
Material: Resins of different colours
Photography: ©Fabrice Gousset
Producer: Galerie kreo

1

2

1

DUEESTUDIO
Claudia & Harry Washington

2008
1 L'Astiko Chair
Material: Stainless steel, rubber tubing
Photography: Harry Washington
Producer: DUEestudio

L'Astiko is part of the Washington's Haute Couture line, which has an eco-friendly focus. The designers were looking for a material that would fit the chair's frame in a chaotic way, but would not compromise functionality and comfort. Using the inner tubes of old tires gave the seat a rugged urban aesthetic.

2008
2 Olga Chair
Material: Stainless steel, leather
Photography: Rodrigo Tablas
Producer: DUEestudio for The Future Perfect

In the *Olga chair*, the stainless steel structures are hand-fitted using the craftsmanship of Salvadoran saddle makers, a vanishing technique. The straps in the rear are intended to resemble a corsage, but they also serve as the structure that bears the weight of the sitter's body.

OMER ARBEL

2008
3 25 Bench
Material: Stainless steel, molded plywood, industrial felt
Photography: Robert Keisure
Producer: Bocci

Conventional upholstery is based on a simple principle: foam is encased in fabric to provide comfort. The *25 bench* eliminates foam from the equation and compensates by providing a vast excess of fabric, which is allowed to fold and pleat haphazardly to create a comfortable seat and back. Over time, the randomly folded pleats will shift as they conform to the human body to create interesting organic patterns.

PUNGA AND SMITH

2007
4 Topo Coffee Table
Material: Kauri plywood, powder-coated mild steel
Photography: Stephen Goodenough

The *Topo Table* is a limited-edition piece that introduces a touch of humour and uncertainty to the living room. *Topo Tables* are produced as one-off pieces and only one edition of each geographic location is manufactured. Clients may request "custom" locations.

2

3

4

For 15 years, the French designers Antoine Audiau and Manuel Warosz, as Antoine+Manuel, have been wildly crossing disciplines to create everything from ad campaigns, fashion shows and 3D sculpture to window displays, wallpapers, decorative stickers and furniture. Antoine, the colourist, and Manuel, a master of layout, are both designers and illustrators, and bring the best qualities of each discipline to the other.

Antoine et Manuel graphics look like constructions; their constructions look like graphics. Invitations for Christian Lacroix fashion shows feature billowing blots, blossoms and teardrops in bright yellow and mint, black and metallic silver, and their patterns are echoed in shapes that are embossed or laser-cut. Their *Troy* wallpaper depicts a mountaintop city: a mythical, cartoonish Arcadia rendered in shades of blue. Another called *Possession* is half-naïve and half high-tech in its style, half tree of life and half circuitboard, with monitor-like buds growing into each other. Are the figures in *Incarnation* totemic or comic? *Hybrid* takes Linnaeus literally, swapping the single purple, pink and orange petals of a plump chrysanthemum with those of a daisy, and vice-versa. Their architectural follies grow things as much as their trees and flowers. Their cities, with safely circumscribed corners, are inhabited by blobular characters. *The Happy Living* installation made an entire environment out of wall-coverings at Taipei's Museum of Tomorrow: white-box galleries were striped with black chevrons, decorated with potted cacti and threaded with illustrations of stairs that run into real doorways.

Cabinet (2008)

The artists' furniture gives dimension to their 2D work –which was already straining the page, ready to burst forth. These reassuring shapes, surreal landscapes and unending connections between creatures and objects also inform their furniture (often made for Paris design shop Domestic): tables, seating, mirrors, credenzas, cabinets and shelves made in acrylic or blond wood, with puddling or doily-like silhouettes, sown with landscapes that are rounded but not wilting, rubberized in form but not in material.

For New York gallery 21st/21st, Antoine and Manuel created *Liteboxes1*, *2* and *3* and a filigreed cabinet cut from black and white acrylic. These miniature architectural objects, complete with arches and latticed screens feature thick chunky chains, contain their electrical cords like chic accessories that recall the handles of Chanel handbags. The lacy three-story cabinet resembles a Jean Prouvé Maison Tropicale bred with an M.C. Escher illustration of lofty Italianate architectural elements leading nowhere but into each other.

Antoine+Manuel's white *Tout Va Bien* credenza for BD Barcelona Design is gouged with deep relief patterns that the designers culled from a smattering of sources: arts and crafts, hieroglyphics, contemporary graphics and fantasy. Again, the artists included the stairs that go (contentedly) nowhere, mixing them with cactuses, rain clouds and mineral facets and perching all of it on impossible, or at least unexpected, conical or spherical feet. Naturally, the *Tout Va Bien* can be fabricated in any shade of the RAL colour reference spectrum. Antoine's doing, no doubt.

www.antoinetmanuel.com

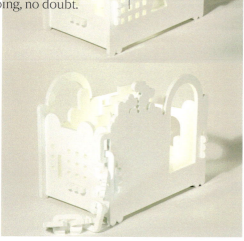

2007
LiteBox 1
Material: Laser-cut perspex
Photography: Antoine+Manuel

ANTOINE
+
MANUEL

2008
Tout Va Bien Sideboard
Producer: BD diciones

ANTOINE+MANUEL
2007
1 La France Table
2 Falaise Shelves
3 Millefeuille Chest
   Material: Lasercut perspex
   Producer: Edith
   Photography: Antoine+Manuel
   Producer: Edith

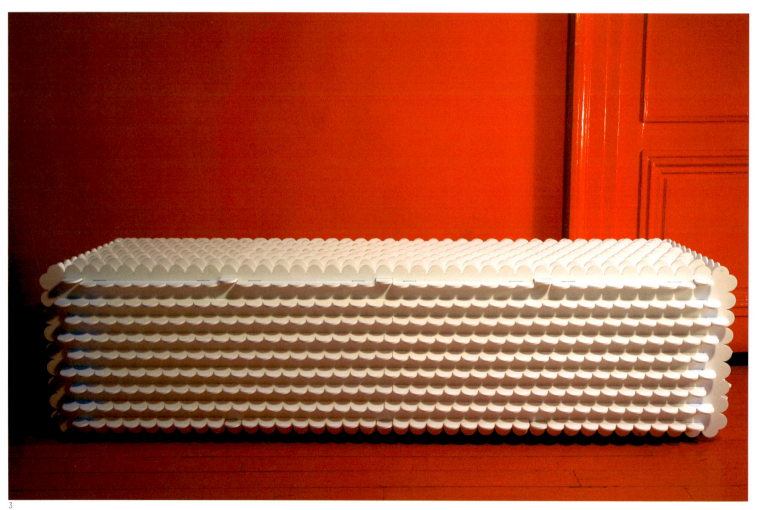

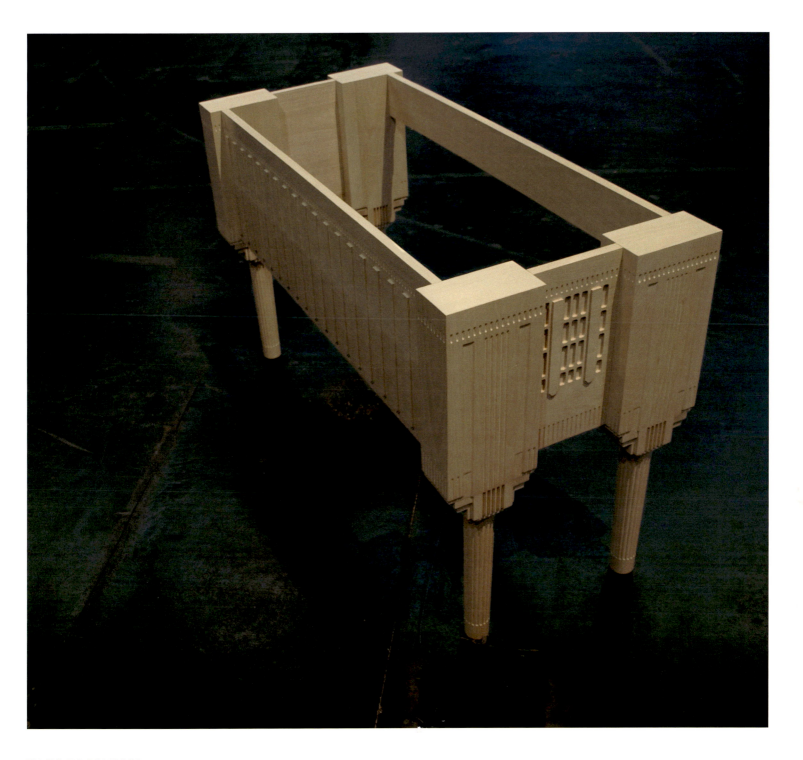

TIAGO DA FONSECA

2008
£250 Million Topless Table
Material: Beech
Photography: Tiago da Fonseca
Producer: Tiago da Fonseca

Battersea Power Station is the largest brick-built structure
in Europe, designed in 1930 by Sir Giles Scott and notable
for its original and lavish Art Deco fittings and décor. Its
familiar four-chimney footprint has since become one of
London's iconic landmarks. Closed since 1983, there have
been several plans to redevelop the station but no action
has ever been taken, turning the site into a commodity that
changes hands frequently with the latest price tag at £250
million. The table and the power station have something in
commom as they await the ultimate intervention.

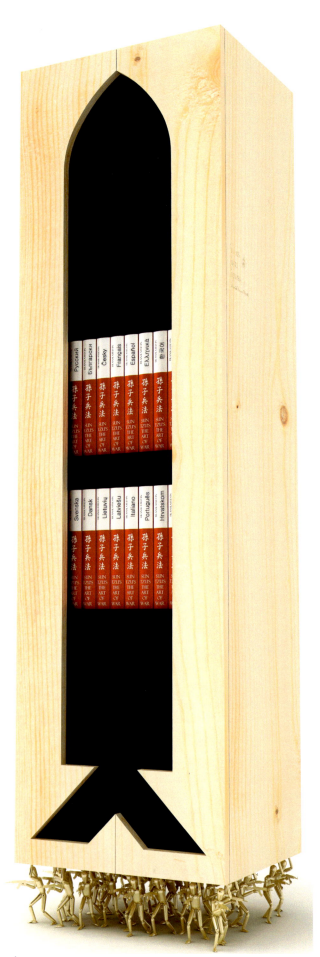

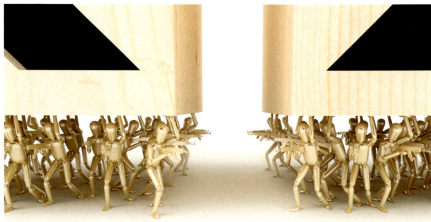

2

DANIEL LOVES OBJECTS

2009
1 Of Wars & Wits & Power Cabinet
Material: Solid wood, powder-coated steel,
gold-plated die-cast aluminium
Photography: Dennis Han

For any country or individual feeling a bit belligerent when asked to disarm or refrain from nuclear missile testing, this bookshelf comes complete with a strategically placed golden army.

2009
2 At Your Command Lamps
Material: Gold-plated die-cast aluminium
Photography: Dennis Han

At Your Command is a classical movable mannequin that has evolved into a lamp. Every movement of the joints is in the user's control.

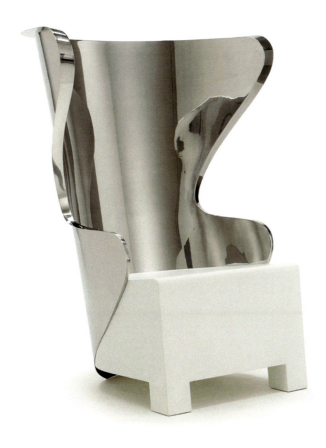

FREDRIKSON STALLARD
Patrik Fredrikson & Ian Stallard

2007
1 Bergère 2 Chair
Material: Stainless steel and rubber
Photography: Thomas Brown,
Courtesy David Gill Galleries
Producer: David Gill Galleries

DUNCAN BULL
Geoff Machen

2008
2 Vase Table
Material: Solid beech, tempered glass,
handblown glass vaser
Producer: ErnestHoward

PHILIPPE BESTENHEIDER

2007
3 Alice Armchair
Material: Golden polished aluminium,
golden anodized clover-leaf elements
Photography: Amendolagine Barracchia
Producer: Nilufar Edition

The Meta furniture line by the legendary London antiques house, Mallett, confirms craft's role as the most important value-adding component of contemporary design. Ironically, this is the company's first contemporary collection. Since 1865, Mallett has been a purveyor of Regency armchairs, Chippendale window seats, Empire day beds and the like. However, led by consulting creative directors Louise-Anne Comeau and Geoffrey Monge, Mallett recruited avant-garde designers – including BarberOsgerby, Tord Boontje, Matali Crasset and so-called digital architects Asymptote – to fabricate modern furniture in collaboration with world-class, and difficult to find, craftsmen wielding 18th-century techniques and materials.

Featured in Meta's inaugural 2008 collection was Asymptote's *Ivy_03* coffee table. Its swagging, slumped-glass surface rests atop an undulating, crimped Tula steel base, the formula of which had to be re-created in an Oxford University laboratory from a rare sample sheet dating back to 1780's Imperial Russia. To produce it, Asymptote worked with craftsmen who had refurbished parts of the Kremlin. Other pieces introduced in 2008 included a blown-glass reading table with integrated lamp by London-based BarberOsgerby, one of the largest pieces ever to be mouth-blown.

The supremely high quality of the work – and corresponding prices – represent an elevation of both design and craft. Drafting the designers was relatively easy, but finding the craftsmen was no small task. Comeau and Monge did historical research and manned the phones to track studios that have maintained a pedigree at the pinnacle of decorative arts. Few have websites. "It took us over a year to source the ateliers, around 50 of them. We sought out the 'maker's maker-of-choice,' if you will," explains Comeau, who sought mastery of pre-production processes for mould-making, sample artwork and material analysis, as well as the production itself. The creative directors met with half a dozen makers before finding one to mould Boontje's double-curved armoire, with its seven layers of veneer. The most difficult material to recreate, for Crasset's diamond-shaped lanterns, was the extinct Paktong metal, unproduced for over 150 years. Although the component elements had been determined at Oxford, the foundry still had to determine precisely how to mix the elements together (the ferrous and non-ferrous blend, in what order, at what temperature, with what type of cooling). Surprisingly, glass often proved difficult to source because modern "float" glass has become de rigueur and poured glass (for the mirrors) seems to have gone extinct. "In general," Comeau admits, "All of the ateliers were difficult to find as the techniques and quality required by us made nearly every request exceptional. And on a few occasions, the ateliers themselves insisted on interviewing us to make sure that our aspirations for the work were as high as their own."

www.madebymeta.com

ASYMPTOTE
Hani Rashid &
Lise-Anne Couture

2008
Ivy_03
Material: Steel,
slumped glass
Photography: Lee Mawdsley for Meta
Producer: Meta

META BY MALLET

ASYMPTOTE
Hani Rashid & Lise-Anne Couture

2008
1 **Mnemos III Snuff Boxes**
   Material: Vermeil, satin, wood
   Photography: Lee Mawdsley for Meta
   Producer: Meta by Mallett

BARBEROSGERBY
Edward Barber & Jay Osgerby

2008
2 **Cidade Candelabra**
   Material: 1958 Britannia silver, pearwood,
   custom-made beeswax candles
4 **Cupola Reading Table and Light**
   Material: Moulded blown glass, free blown
   glass, white bronze Carrara marble
   Photography: Lee Mawdsley for Meta
   Producer: Meta by Mallett

MATALI CRASSET

2008
3 **Diamonds Are a Girl's Best Friend Lanterns**
   Material: Paktong — based upon analysis
   of an 18th century Chinese paktong can-
   dlestick by Oxford University's Archaeologi-
   cal Material Sciences Unit.
   Hand-blown glass panes
   Photography: Lee Mawdsley for Meta
   Producer: Meta

TORD BOONTJE

2008

1 L'Armoire
Material: Cocobolo, mahogany, padouk
Photography: Lee Mawdsley for Meta
Producer: Meta by Mallett

2008

3 The Fig Leaf Wardrobe
Material: Hand-painted enamel,
bronze, silk
Photography: Lee Mawdsley for Meta
Producer: Meta by Mallett

This wardrobe's monumental *fig-leaf* encrusted doors open to reveal a bronze tree arching up and outward against the background of a tranquil silk landscape. Each wardrobe requires 616 hand-painted enamel leaves, the largest project of its kind in history. A special method of supporting them was developed, so that no clamp marks would be visible. The overall size of the larger leaves as well as the enormous surface area to be painted, was originally thought to be impossible to enamel. Each leaf is signed on the underside by the craftsman, numbered and recorded. The tracery structure was created by Atelier de Forge, a traditional iron foundry in rural France. Inside grows a life-like bronze tree, which was cast using the lost-wax process and created by Patrick Blanchard, head of sculpture at the École Boulle, Paris. The wardrobe includes eight matching bronze hangers. The patination of the bronze was overseen by Chevillard, a specialist in metals founded in 1850.

PATRICK BLANCHARD

2008

2 Acanthus Table Lamps
Material: Lime, sycamore woods
Photography: Clive Bartlett
Producer: Meta by Mallett

2

1

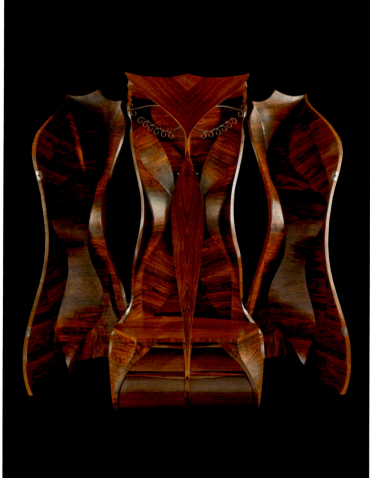

3

2008
VanityTidy XL Bowl
Material: Black translucent resin,
stereolythography
Photography: Daniel Schweizer
Producer: Tools Galerie

1

2

DITTE HAMMERSTROEM

2008
1 Bunch of Boxes Cabinet
Material: Lacquered MDF, black rope
Photography: Jeppe Gudmundsen-Holmgreen

A hanging cabinet consisting of a series of small boxes, which can be expanded to include additional boxes whenever one is in need of more storage space.

LABEL OBJET
Francis Chabloz

2008
2 Stereolego Vase
Material: Stereolithography
Photography: Tonatiuh Ambrosetti

This vase eschews the popular codes of Lego, abandoning the innocence of the world of the children to which it is attached. By sexualising the object, the designer gives it a (very adult) function. A profusion of iconic images gives the object a face with multiple characters, allowing the viewer to catch glimpses of several sources of inspiration, from Goldorak and Art-Toys to Totem.

1

LELLO//ARNELL
Jørgen Craig Lello & Tobias Arnell

2008
1 **Gentleman's Traveling Shrine**
Material: Antique chairs, porcelain, silver,
crystal, wood, shrink-wrap
Photography: Niklas Lello,
www.niklaslello.com

2008
2 **Dr. Livingstone or: How I Learned to Stop
Worrying and Love the World**
Material: First edition of H.M. Stanleys
Photography: Niklas Lello

2008
3 **Taking One Step Back in Order to
Take Two Steps Forward**
Material: Varnished world globe
(cardboard, brass and wood)
Photography: Niklas Lello

2

3

1

2

3

4

5

6

LIANA YAROSLAVSKY

2008
1 L'Esquisse Coffee Table
Photography: Cecil Mathieu

2009
2 O2 Variation Coffee Table
Photography: Cecil Mathieu

2008
3 Dome Coffee Table
Photography: Cecil Mathieu

2008
4 Decadence
Photography: Cecil Mathieu

2009
5 Maure de Venise Coffee Table
Photography: Cecil Mathieu

2008
6 Pluie Coffee Table
Photography: Cecil Mathieu

1

2

3

4

SHI JIANMIN

2007
1 **Suckling Piglets Table**
Material: Bronze
Photography: Shi Jianmin and
gabrielle ammann//gallery

SATYENDRA PAKHALÉ

2007/08
2 **Bell Metal Table**
Material: Bronze
Photography: The artist and
gabrielle ammann//gallery
Producer: gabrielle ammann//gallery

2007/08
3 **Bell Metal Chair**
Material: Bronze with sandblasted
surface coating
Photography: The artist and
gabrielle ammann//gallery
Producer: gabrielle ammann//gallery

SEBASTIAN BRAJKOVIC

2009
4 **Lathe Table**
Material: Aluminium
Photography: Sebastian Brajkovic
Producer: Sebastian Brajkovic

AUTOBAN
Seyhan Özdemir & Sefer Çağlar

2008
5 **Spider Light**
Material: Stainless steel or
gold-plated steel
Producer: De La Espada

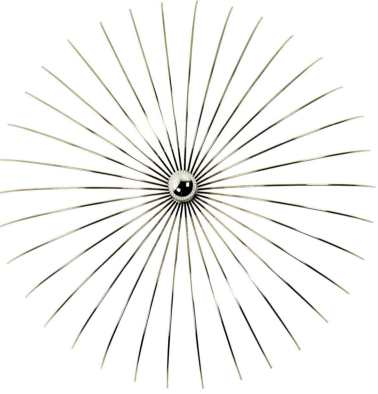

5

2008
1 **Industry Centerpiece on Pedestal**
  Material: dyed tulip tree, dyed bird's-eye maple,
  bronze, 24k gilding
2 **Industry Cabinet**
  Material: dyed tulip tree, dyed bird's-eye maple
  Photography: R. Kot, Brussels
  Producer: Studio Job
  Collection Mitterrand + Cramer, Geneva

1

2

LOUISE HINDSGAVL

2009
1 **Silence! In the Event of a Divine Presence Figurines**
Material: Porcelain, rope, aluminum
Producer: Danish Crafts

PIET BOON ZONE

2009
2 **Hot Kroon Chandelier**
Photography: D. Brandsma

An 18-arm chandelier manually dripped with polyurethane to make each piece unique.

EMMEMOBILI

2009
3 **Tuileries Table**
Material: Metal, glass
Producer: Emmemobili

1

2

PHILIPPE BESTENHEIDER

2009
1 Lui 6 Armchair
Material: Wood, fabric
Producer: Fratelli Boffi

2009
2 Lui 5 Armchair
Material: Wood, handwoven caning
Producer: Fratelli Boffi

2009
3 Lui 6 Sofa
Material: Fabric
Producer: Fratelli Boffi

3

BOCA DO LOBO
Pedro Sousa

2008
1   Gold LeBIO I/GO Folding Screen
Material: Glass fiber
Photography: Pedro Saraiva
Producer: Boca do Lobo

1

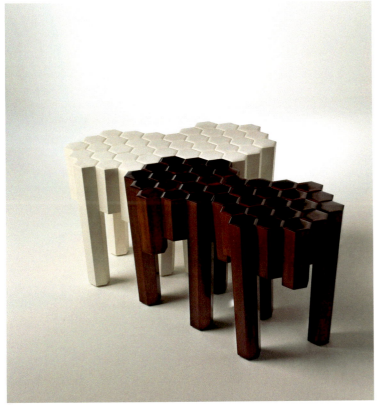

PHILIPPE BESTENHEIDER

2009
2   Lui 6 Stools
Material: Glossy mahogany
or bleached maple finish
Photography: Fratelli Boffi
Producer: Fratelli Boffi

Bestenheider's stools are made of wooden blocks with a hexagonal cross-section, creating a beehive system that enables them to be used singly or in groups, and makes them suitable for public spaces.

2

BOCA DO LOBO
Pedro Sousa

2008
1 Mondrian Sideboard
Material: Wood, glass, fabric
Photography: Pedro Saraiva
Producer: Boca do Lobo

2008
2 Victoria Cupboard
Material: Glass, wood, fabric
Photography: Pedro Saraiva
Producer: Boca do Lobo

2008
3 D. Manuel Cupboard
Material: Wood, copper leaf
Photography: Pedro Saraiva
Producer: Boca do Lobo

2008
4 Diamond Sideboard
Material: Wood, silver and gold leaf
Photography: Pedro Saraiva
Producer: Boca do Lobo

Sousa's opulent tribute to the unmistakable and signature Portuguese style dubbed Manuelino.

1

2

3

4

Hunting and gathering

If iconic design really does meet its mortal end,___

___ the turnaround will probably be felt most acutely in places where it once recorded its greatest triumphs

And surely enough, in the galleries and art fairs where the high mass of the icon was being celebrated only recently, where even the taps once glittered in gold and the air was imbued with incense and myrrh, a new modesty has begun to take hold. It is not the kind of modesty that rubs off on the prices of the objects or that even questions the system of art and design hybrids. The self-doubt of designers does not extend that far. No, the new modesty finds expression in a new form, in topics that appear more suited to the times than the hysterical presence and the superficial luxuriousness that had shaped the dimension of visual appearance in recent years.

Juxtaposing

A variety of different formal currents and ideas can be subsumed under this new modesty. The only thing that unites them is an orientation towards the clumsy handcraft of archaic societies, coupled with a certain coarseness that one can search for in vain in the design of civilised nations. In short: designers who until recently were regarded as the epitome of the reincarnated Baroque figure are now roaming the land as hunters and gatherers. A contradiction? By no means. In some sense this is all happening at the same time. The Baroque figure and the primitive hunter may have nothing formal in common, but in certain

Makkink & Bey (2009)

ways they are two expressions of the same creative type who – as if the two hemispheres of the brain had become separated – manages to delight two parallel universes with his/her work. They lie in close proximity and yet exist in total independence of one another.

Archaic nature

The search for the prototype, the beginning of all design, informs a whole series of contemporary objects. These play with grand gestures, with that leap in evolutionary history which first inspired us humans to stand up and allowed us to become artisans and warriors. The tone is set by furniture hewn

Max Lamb (2008)

from stone – like the monolith of knowledge that American director Stanley Kubrick presented to early man to make him aware of himself in the *2001* odyssey. The crudeness of the form is part of the agenda: indeed the cruder the better. The resulting objects are not chairs but thrones – formed for ancient rulers. The tool of choice is the hand axe. Universal in purpose, it can even be used to skin animals if the hide is needed. In a totally negligent or perhaps deliberately provocative manner, skins and hides are thrown over metal skeletons. Everything breathes intensity. Aside from the form, the materials used are responsible for creating this impression. They are purely natural materials, often untreated or confronted with techniques from primordial times. Leather, for example, is boiled until it can be warped into shape over a three-dimensional template before stabilising itself. The timber used is at least 1000 years old. Cracks and splits are visible and the grain can be read like a book. Another element to reappear in design is rusty Corten steel that we previously encountered in the gigantic sculpture of Richard Senna. On a human scale, the Serra sculpture is converted into a stool. Behind all these forms of expression is the desire to live in Arcadia – an unspoilt, self-contained garden of paradise. In the field of architecture, a new chalet culture that experiments with new forms of rusticness has already taken root. Like design, it draws on folkloristic images of nature without actually displaying them. This archaic nature positively celebrates the natural quality and sensuality of the materials, entirely devoting itself to the apparently innate human yearning for sensuous experience. After all, primal instincts can be wonderfully concealed behind the archaic façade.

Shapeless – the new ugly

Once the instincts have been acted out, the designers can turn to their favourite objects: the unspectacular things of everyday life. These too have something archaic about them, just that archaic here refers not to the early period of handcraft but to industrial production. They are things that people once genuinely needed; things that were once incredibly useful but whose existence people now

Robert Stadler (2009)

only notice when they suddenly need them, only to discover that they have disappeared from the market altogether due to their increasingly blatant uselessness. But designers harbour a deep love for these things, which is why they are dragged into the glare of public attention with incredible regularity. Sometimes in the form of icon making, like the exaggerated concept of the super normal – an art term that for a while seemed capable of drawing sufficient attention to the everyday. At other times in the form of presentations that are intended to tease out the emotional side of these everyday objects – basically to breathe some personality into their impersonal appearance. The latter seems to be veritably blooming at present. But if we take at face value all the flabby and pot-bellied forms, the dripping light bulbs and buckled cutlery that are currently dominating the scene, the emotional state of everyday design does not appear to be in particularly good shape. Indeed, this new slackness represents a provocation in contrast to the hardened and permanently aligned bodies that were once pressed out of the machine

and mechanically lined up on the conveyor belt. The design here is carried out with the attitude of refusal and in clear opposition to the notion of formal innovation. Instead the designers seek refuge in falling back on basic shapes, on generic design that conjures up the impression of always having been there. And it is not confined to product design: the rediscovery of apparently simple typefaces such as Helvetica and Futura in contemporary communication design feels like an absolute revelation. This world of primordial forms is not suspected of aesthetic aging. In fact it is considered to be timeless – even though it has returned at regular intervals throughout the entire history of industrial design.

Soft-edged

What the Austrian artist Erwin Wurm presented a few years ago with his *Fat Car* – a Porsche gone out of shape – seems to have developed into a widespread obesity throughout the everyday world. Is it actually a critique of the outmoded nature of the industrially-manufactured product? Or is it merely about providing the forgotten little helpers with a new form of presence? Perhaps the slumped and flagging state of the

Brodie Neil (2009)

forms is a purely aesthetic response to the pumped up and bristling formal world of recent years. Letting the air out can have an extremely liberating effect – not just on the semantic level. No, new possibilities are also opening up for forms. The undefined, imprecise element is assuming a naturalness that purports to accept no limits. Virus-like interventions leave their genetic fingerprints everywhere and lend our static object world an unimagined and presumably destructive vitality. But that the unstable can also possess a certain athleticism is demonstrated by designs which play with the static in a different way. These include chair legs that have been deliberately made slightly too thin, thereby elevating the wobbling of the object to a self-stabilising principle. From the apparently flawed, we can develop a positively orthopaedic argument: shades here of Darwin and his theory of only the fittest surviving.

Hard-edged

But things can also be different: alongside the bulging, the wobbling and the uncontrollable leaking of forms, the precision of the canted

surface is asserting itself. It sends out a message of archaic dimensions because the simplicity of the folded iron or steel shape remains unsurpassed. It is the prototype of intelligence, and in times of new modesty it is scaling new heights. From

DesignRethink & Development (2008)

surface to form – via the principle of folding – this approach has spawned a veritable arsenal of contemporary designs. Sometimes they appear in the aesthetic of American stealth bombers, despite being just water taps. Sometimes they use the material intensity of rusted steel to carry the formal message of hard edge to greater extremes.

Pixel park

But the fact that the transition from surface to form can look different in the digital age than it did in the industrial and pre-industrial past without necessarily sacrificing the desired rudimentary or coarse appearance is beyond dispute. It is no great shock that the increased mixing of the virtual and real worlds has also been seized upon

as a topic by the hunters and gatherers. Perfectly befitting the desire for archaic form and archaic expression, the focus here is on the coarsening of reality by the virtual image. Countless objects and pieces of furniture are currently being made that look like enlarged 72dpi photographs that have been projected into the third dimension. Like a digital image, they appear to be composed of individual pixels – except that these pixels are made from wood rather than data. In this way, the virtual element is transformed into something physical and tangible.

We return at the end to the material level of design. It is physical presence that ultimately keeps us grounded in an opaque world with a less than clear future. If the immaterial level of design reserves an exclusive right to the management of meaning, ultimately becoming a matter of individual interpretation, the material level is assigned to human instinct. And its significance is set to grow – at least in the ongoing flirtation between art and design.

Pepe Heykoop (2009)

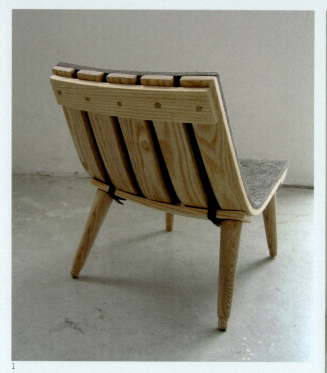

BOOKHOU
John Booth

2008
1 Child's Felt Chair
Material: Steam bent ash, felt
Producer: bookhou

PATRICIA URQUIOLA

2008
2 Vieques Bathtub
Material: Steel tub, teak,
Photography: Agape
Producer: Agape

TOMÁS ALONSO

2009
3 5° Stool
Material: Wood, alpine rope
Producer: Nils Holger Moormann
Photography: Nils Holger Moormann

SCOTT GARCIA

2007
1 Process Chair
Material: Sycamore
Photography: Scott Garcia
Producer: Scott Garcia

This chair tells a clear narrative about man's willingness to subvert nature, regardless of the potential environmental and social costs. It comments on consumerism, supermarket culture and the ways in which today's shopper has been alienated from the processes used to change raw materials into the objects we use every day. "Most people look at a steak and think of it with chips rather than legs," Garcia notes. In *Process*, a secondary sycamore branch has been carved into the chair's back leg with the last section left unworked. The rest of the seat follows an understated, archetypal form.

MARCO DESSI

2009
2 Prater Chair
Material: Plywood
Photography: Tobias Schlorhaufer
Producer: Richard Lampert

FREDRIKSON STALLARD

Patrik Fredrikson & Ian Stallard

3 Table #1 (Log)
Material: Wood, steel
Photography: Thomas Brown/Courtesy
David Gill Galleries
Producer: David Gill Galleries

1

2

3

1

PETER MARIGOLD

2008
1 Thin Slice Cabinet
Material: Eucalyptus, oak, ply
Photography: Peter Marigold
Producer: Gallery Libby Sellers

This series is named for a psychological term describing the human capacity to discern vast amounts of information from a relatively small amount of data. For this cabinet, Marigold laid out cross sections of each wood in the sequence in which each section was cut, revealing the trees' growth patterns. *Thin Slice* riffs on Marigold's fascination with altered geometry's capacity to change our perception of the objects around us. In order to "amplify" the logic of the natural world, he emphasises nature's forms while inverting its structures, asking us to see things we usually miss.

TOM DE VRIEZE

2008
2 La MDF Stool
Material: Medium density fibreboard
Photography: Tom de Vrieze
Producer: Sixinch

Indoor stool made from slats glued and fastened together that will rock when tipped forward slightly.

2

STUDIO NIELS & SVEN

2008
1 Wooden BBQ
Material: Wood
Producer: Studio Niels & Sven

2009
2 1000 Chairs Chair
Material: Wood
Producer: Studio Niels & Sven

A refinement of the collage aesthetic that mixes old design classics to create a new one.

BO YOUNG JUNG & EMMANUEL WOLFS

2009
3 Tree Trunk Chair
Material: Bronze
Producer: gabrielle ammann // gallery
Photography: gabrielle ammann // gallery

BCXSY

2009
CHANGE! Furniture Series
Material: Polyurethane foam, rubber coat
Photography: Jakob Hohmann
Producer: BCXSY

1

JASON MILLER

2009
1 Woolly Chair
Material: Industrial felt, polyester, brass, bison hide
Producer: Jason Miller Studio

Woolly is made almost entirely of animal hair, with a structure folded and sewn from industrial wool felt and an outer cover of bison hide. Like a bear rug or a Native American robe, a tanned hide is used whole, making *Woolly* a decadent chair.

BCXSY

2009
2 Stone Stool
Material: PU foam, PU rubber coating, memory foam
3 Boulder Shelf
Material: PU foam, PU rubber coating
4 Squeeze Light
Material: PU foam, PU rubber coating, LED light
Photography: BCXSY
Producer: BCXSY

A furniture and home accessories series constructed from rubber-coated foam. Beyond the Stone Age aesthetics, the material makes each piece appear hard and heavy, but actually renders each resilient, flexible and lightweight. While many foam products are machine-cut, BCXSY CNC milled blocks of it, but then cut them by hand, making each piece unique. The designers used different densities of different foam pieces, giving the collection both softness and structure.

2   3   4

The product, furniture, interior design and micro-architecture of Jürgen Bey and wife Rianne Makkink of Rotterdam-based Studio Makkink & Bey often tell tales. Bey has long been known for exploring everything from the fabric of cities, the habits of waiting and even dust in order to create objects that conform to the way we actually live or would like to live. Today, the studio's curiosity about the relationship between people and things drives the clarity, freshness and lyricism of its work.

In early 2008, Makkink & Bey transformed a stack of wooden 2x4s and a long bolt of wool felt into a temporary home at La Galerie de Pierre Bergé & Associés. The *Witness Flat* was patched together using felt swatches and wood slats, to create improvised furniture like a stuffed straight-back chair, a desk with an integrated chandelier, two armchairs that were pixelated images of them-

Detail

selves, and a traditional spindle-back chair trussed in a chunky knit "sweater" that exposes the "skin" of two legs and one arm. The following year, the Bergé Gallery also commissioned Makkink and Bey to make a unique seating series that reinterprets Brazilian design. The result was one-off wood-and-leather chairs that use ash or American walnut instead of the recently protected Brazilian hardwoods, and that play, almost humorously, with the proportions of component parts while adding the designers' own contemporary pixelated aesthetic.

In 2009, Bey collaborated with new Dutch office furnishings company, Prooff, to bring his rethinking of banal rituals to the workspace under the rubric "Progressive Office." Prooff presented Bey's *Ear Chair*<small>p. 74</small> and the provocatively named *Work Sofa* in Milan, along with the *Slow Chair*, originally a concept for Vitra, which enclosed the employee inside what looks like a computer monitor (with just as focused a view

outwards) atop a task chair on road tires which lets them "drive" at up to 40 km/h, a speed limit intended to allow them to slow down and focus, in both literal and figurative ways. Bey calls it "the best office chair and not the slowest car."

Also in 2009, the 15-year-old Dutch conceptual design company, Droog, hired the pair to create its latest New York City shop. Makkink and Bey chose to expose the old brick walls and then dress them scantily in sheer curtains with pixelated graphics that run in meandering tracks along the ceiling, offering reconfigurable partitioning. The interior's factory-like brick and skylights contrast neatly with Studio Makkink & Bey's *House of Blue*, a small single-story structure that gives ballast to the space, as a whole. The designers CNC-milled the slim profile of a nearly full-scale home from stiff but lightweight polyurethane foam to be sold in cross-sections (replete with domestic details: creeping ivy, a working chimney, a picket fence) or sold as a whole that can be customized to the client's own interior. The *House* generates a backdrop for merchandise while becoming merchandise itself. Makkink and Bey also designed another series of products, small coffee tables and chairs routed from flat panels and assembled by fitting slats into slots, the waste material of which is used to build walls downstairs and a banister on the steps. Now that they've studied our old habits, the designers appear poised to teach us new ones.

www.jurgenbey.nl

MAKKINK & BEY

2008
BRAZIL INFLUENCE MEETS BRAZIL STYLE

Brazilian design and interpretations by
Studio Makkink & Bey

1

JO MEESTERS

2008
1 PULP Vessels
   Material: Paper, glue, resin
   Photography: Lisa Klappe
   Producer: Studio Jo Meesters

PULP is a collection of vessels made from paper pulp, salvaging discarded vessels to create a positive mould. Using newspaper, glue and water, a paste is applied over the outer surface of the mould. After repeating the same process, the dried vessel is removed from the mould by cutting it in two, gluing it together again before then applying the last layers of the *paste*. Meesters then treated the vessel with an inner epoxy resin coating. The collection began as a search for alternative materials made of paper waste. By combining other materials with paper pulp (epoxy resin, glues), a new material is born that, though made of paper, can hold water.

2004
2 Ornamental Inheritance Vessels
   Material: Used ceramics
   Photography: Lisa Klappe
   Producer: Studio Jo Meesters

Meesters sand-blasted used ceramic vases to create *Ornamental Inheritance*. Combining contemporary symbols, such as airplanes, nature and architecture, in combination with traditional Delftware decoration, creates a modern legacy.

2005
3 Botanical Vessels
   Material: Nylon
4 Allium Sativum Vase
   Material: Porcelain

2006
5 A String Of Garlic Vase
   Material: Porcelain
   Photography: Jo Meesters
   Producer: Studio Jo Meesters in collaboration with Marije van der Park and Willem Derks

2

3

4

5

POSTFOSSIL

Anna Blattert & Daniel Gafner

2009
1 Sabooh & Mitsu Lamps
Material: Oak wood, porcelain, gold
Photography: Miriam Graf
Producer: Postfossil

The lamps Sabooh and Mitsu demonstrate that energy-saving LED technology can, and should, be used in the home. Based on oriental lanterns, their translucent porcelain shades give a warm, diffuse light. The golden decoration on the inner shade serves as a reflector, as well as a conductor from cable to bulb. By lightly pulling the hanging cable, the shade can be swung through 360°.

Thomas Walde

2009
2 Charcoal Pile Table
Material: Oiled oak, glass
Photography: Miriam Graf
Producer: Postfossil

Oiled oak pieces ranged in a circle and "wood-welded" are held together without glue to form the base of this table. Its shape is reminiscent of the conically stacked wood piles used in charcoal burning. The work takes as its central theme this energy source, a precursor of fossil fuel, and is meant to stimulate thought about future sources of energy.

1

2

POSTFOSSIL
Claudia Heiniger

2009
1 **Bivano Seat for Two**
Material: Wood, elastic, wool felt
Photography: Miriam Graf
Producer: Postfossil

A space-saving couch, the frame of which consists of multilayer boards cut from a single panel during production. The printed felt belts stand in symbolically for the cushioning that is completely absent in *Bivano*.

Florian Hauswirth

2009
2 **Loppa Lamp**
Material: Paper, natural glue
Photography: Miriam Graf
Producer: Postfossil

This lamp wraps its bulb the way an envelope encloses a letter. The paper it is made from is creased into a robust structure with the flaps folded upwards, one side moistened before both are joined. These connecting ribs give the filigree lampshade its stability. Its energy-saving bulb, which will soon become the lighting standard, generates less heat while the piece's flat shape enables easy transport.

2009
5 **JWC (Just Wood Chair)**
Material: 100% beechwood
Photography: Miriam Graf
Producer: Postfossil

This chair is constructed from unglued wood, its joints connected via a new wood-joining technique called "rotation dowel welding." The heat generated by placing the dowels releases adhesives present in the wood – lignin and hemicellulose – forming a substantial welded bond in seconds. The design was produced in collaboration with Sebastian Kraft of the Biel School for Wood Technology (BFH – AHB).

2009
3 **Plymet Stool / Side Table**
Material: Anodised aluminium
Photography: Miriam Graf
Producer: Postfossil

A stool or side table that folds into shape from a flat form.

Christine Birkhoven

2009
4 **Souffleur Ramon Fireside Set**
Material: Wood, leather, stainless steel
Photography: Miriam Graf
Producer: Postfossil

This fireside companion set comprises a bellows and a firewood basket. A bellows is not only a beautiful object with a homely character, but also a reflection of the energy needed to kindle a fire. Bellows have been fading into obscurity, either due to modern heating technology or because there are quicker methods of ignition today (such as firelighters). But firelighters are often unhealthy and environmentally unfriendly. This design is intended to breathe new life into the bellows while saving resources.

1

4

2

3

5

ATELIER NL
Nadine Sterk, Lonny van Ryswyck

2008
Drawn from Clay Series Ceramics
1 **Polderceramics, Patato Bowl and Jug**
2 **Polderceramics, Tulip Vase Blanc H104,**
   Bulb Vase K13
Material: Earthenware
Photography: Paul Scala
Styling: Lucas van Vugt

Artists have long explored the significance of place: as a site of history and identity; as a dynamic process in constant flux; and as a politically charged vehicle for both challenging and contextualising the world. For Eindhoven-based Atelier NL, the place was the Noordoostpolder region of the central Netherlands. At the invitation of Jurgen Bey and Rianne Makkink the designers took up residence in the area to better study its social and agricultural character. Since the Noordoostpolder was integral to the Dutch land reclamation acts of the twentieth century (intended to improve flood protection and convert additional land for agriculture) the area is historically and geologically diverse. The studio's

Drawn From Clay series embodies local distinctions as each piece was made from a specific plot of soil taken from area farms dispersed across the 460 -square-kilometre polder. As Sterk explains: "A bucket filled with earth is anonymous, but the stories of the farmer who works the earth lends it its identity." The overriding principal behind the series was to keep the symbiosis between object and origin as clean as possible. The result is tableware that allows the vegetables prepared for dinner to be served in vessels made from the same soilfrom which the vegetables. were taken. The designers refined then mixed each individual batch of soil with water to form malleable clays, before cast-moulding each piece at a consistent temperature in order to compare and contrast the colour and texture of the various soils.The studio also devised a systematic ratio system to determine the size of each piece and stamped each with a "geo-code" to indicate the plot from which the soil was harvested, rendering visible the close relationship between vegetation and clay and, hence, between origin and identity..

ALON MERON

2007
1 Twig Light
Material: Wood, copper, light ampules
Photography: Alon Meron
Producer: Alon Meron

STUDIO LO

2006
2 Ginza Scenography
Material: Felt
Photography: Studio Lo

SAM BARON
Valentina Carretta for Fabrica

2008
3 Floating Flora Glassware
Material: Handmade blown glass
Photography: Gustavo Millon/Fabrica
Producer: SecondoMe

Glass lends a surreal sense of lightness to this branch, the composition of which is reminiscent of the seasons. The piece recalls both a spring bloom or a branch frozen in winter, on which flowers continue to blossom magically.

DECODE
t i m

2009
4 Bell Tables
Material: Polyproylene and ultra-clear glass
Producer: Decode

The *Bell tables* investigate the structural properties of sheet plastic used as surface lamination. The table folds out to form a sturdy matrix that is six times its original volume. The sweeping interior of each tables is shaped by the contours of brass vessels giving an otherwise two dimensional material an unexpected and fluid three dimensional form.

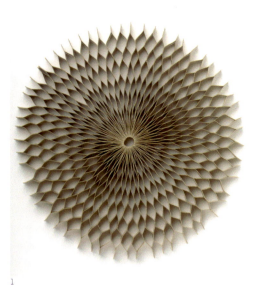

1

3

2

NOSIGNER

2007
1 En Pot Vase
  Material: Paper
  Photography: HATTA
  Producer: Nosigner
  Collection of London Design Museum

A paper pot whose shape changes from a cruet size stick to a disk of 20 cm in diameter.

2007
2 Arborism Table
  Material: Stainles steel
  Photography: HATTA

The branching organic shape of the table base was generated by the fractal algorithm called "Tree Curve" which simulates the growth of a tree.

MARK PRODUCT
Tom Raffield

2009
3 Ribbon Light
  Material: Ash, walnut
  Photography: Kirstin Prisk
  Producer: MARK

Using traditional steam-bending techniques, Raffield made a pendant light with an unusual looping character..

1

BDDW
Tyler Hays

1 **Slab Table**
   Material: Claro walnut,
   hand-rubbed oil finish
2 **Square Guest Armchair**
   Material: American black
   walnut with hand-rubbed
   dark oil finish
3 **Chall Hall Table**
   Material: Claro walnut, live
   edge and Claro walnut joinery
4 **Flower Bed**
   Material: Osage orange wood,
   hand-rubbed oil finish
5 **Lake Side Table**
   Material: White lacquer,
   oxidized maple

2

4

3

5

1

2

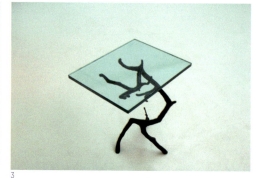

3

4

ONZE STUDIO
Erica Vermeij & Zo Alderfer Ryan

2008/2009

1 **Redefining X Table**
   Material: Hand-finished steel base, American Walnut top
   Producer: LOL (Lots of Lines) Line

2 **Tree Sittin' Bar Stool**
   Material: American Walnut swivel seat, hand cast-aluminum
   Producer: Genesis Line

3 **Genesis End Table**
   Material: Hardened glass, hand-cast bronze
   Producer: Genesis Line

4 **Genesis II End Table**
   Material: White lacquered MDF top Hand cast bronze base
   Producer: Genesis Line

5 **Miro's Lines End Table**
   Material: Lacquered MDF, welded steel
   Producer: LOL (Lots of Lines) Line

6 **Forest Thru the Trees Bench**
   Material: Solid wenge, hand-cast aluminum
   Producer: Genesis Line

6

5

ONZE STUDIO
Erica Vermeij & Zo Alderfer Ryan

2008/2009
1 **Frenchy I Table**
   Material: Antique French door, steel base
   Producer: Found Objects Line
2 **Capital Awry Floor Lamp**
   Material: Antique teak capital base, Plex-
   iglas stem
   Producer: Found Objects Line
3 **Frenchy II End Table**
   Material: Antique French door, steel base
   Producer: Found Objects Line

1

3

2

Archaic Nature

MARIO BOTTA

2009
Kauri Table
Material: Kauri millenarian swamp wood
(ca. 30.240 years old)
Producer: Riva 1920

The Kauri conifer is the largest and most famous of the native trees of New Zealand and grows only in subtropical climates in the north of the country. Approximately 50.000 years ago, natural disasters occurring toward the end of the glacial period, razed entire forests, submerging them in water and mud. The particular characteristics of that mud, together with a lack of oxygen, protected the wood against the chemical process of decomposition, preserving it.

Max Lamb hails from Cornwall. The influence of this accident of birth on the character of Lamb's furniture and product design cannot be underestimated. Its elemental nature is a result of the designer's fascination with, and domination of, natural materials – carving, moulding, smelting, chiselling – and his elaboration of a technical means to do so. The designer brings together industrial production and hand craftsmanship whether he is working with quarried stone, molten metal cast in sand – or potato foam.

Lamb graduated from Northumbria University in 2003 with a degree in Three-Dimensional Design. While studying for his Master's degree (Design Products) at the Royal College of Art, he continued a long-standing project that began with his shaving a stool out of a solid block of polystyrene and fortifying the resulting seat with polyurethane rubber. This is when Lamb began to gel his particular process-driven approach to design through an ongoing project he has dubbed *Exercises in Seating*, which features material and production experiments and includes stools in pewter, copper, laser-sintered polyamide, and armchairs in both polystyrene and 29-gauge stainless steel sheet folded along exaggerated perforations.

After graduating in 2006, Lamb debuted his *Poly Chair*, along with a series of roughly rendered tables, stools, dining and armchairs. He also began developing limited-edition furniture for Tom Dixon, including the CU29 electroformed-copper armchair, the *Silver Slab* dining table and the extruded plastic *Fresh Fat Micro-Factory* chair.

The designer struck out on his own in 2007, fabricating the *Hexagonal Pewter* stool by pouring hot, liquid pewter into incisions made with a small knife into the briny dark sands of the Cornish seashore. The designer then concocted a lounge chair from the froth generated by potato starch extruded into thick, sticky noodles, and moulded. Its ingredients – perhaps a more fitting term than materials – fated the *Starch Chair* for use outdoors where it may be left to compost as summer cools into fall.

SheetSteelTable (2008)

Lamb's deep interest in materials and process means that he researches techniques both sophisticated and rudimentary. Travelling to areas rich in craft (China, Nigeria, India), the Brit feeds his passion to unite local, skill-based industry with emerging high-tech processes. Lamb has cleaved a small series of seating from blocks of quarried lime and sandstone and expanded polystyrene (subsequently cast in bronze or sheathed in rubber). He has mounted 18 chunks of concrete onto a wood-turning lathe, and turned them by hand to create stools. The effect ranges from crude and sweetly cartoonish to classical. Clearly, this designer is as much lion as he is lamb.

www.maxlamb.org

2009
1 **Flat Iron Chair**
   Material: Laser-cut 3mm
   mild steel, zinc plated with
   trivalent passivate

2007/08/09 – ongoing
2 **Scrap Poly Chair**
   Material: Low density expanded polystyrene (EPS),
   high density polyurethane
   rubber coating

1

2

2009
China Granite Project
Material: Chinese green and black granite

A range of furniture pieces including chairs, stools, and low tables cut from raw Chinese granite boulders. Each boulder was hand selected directly from the quarry in Hebei Province, 250 miles South West of Beijing, and cut using a 2.5m diameter diamond blade circular saw. Each cut surface was then polished.

MAX
LAMB

STEPHAN VEIT

2008
1 **Figura Side Table Family**
Material: Massivholz Nussbaum
Producer: Draenert

LEE BORTHWICK

2008
2 **The Take a Seat Outside Collection**
Material: Norway maple, acrylic mirror
3 **The Take a Seat Outside Collection**
Material: Styrene, found tree log,
partially biodegraded

MOTOKI YOSHIO

2007
4 **Blakony Associated Sculpture**
Material: Ceramic

MARK BRAUN

2009
5 **Ö Jewel Cases**
Material: porcelain, gold, platinum
Photography: Inka Recke

RIJADA
Rihards Funts, Peteris Buks

2008

1 Cool Towers Vases
Material: Concrete
Photography: Valdis Jansons
Producer: RIJADA

These 100% concrete vases – whose shapes were inspired by nuclear power station cooling towers – allow users to cultivate a kitchen garden in the kitchen.

TOMAS KRAL

2008

2 Collection Plug - Table lamp
3 Collection Plug - Lamp
4 Collection Plug - Side table
5 Collection Plug - Blue boxes
6 Collection Plug - Bowls
7 Collection Plug - Triple Suspension Lamp
Material: Cork, free-blown glass
Photography by Michel Bonvin
Master degree project at ECAL

Plug is a collection of objects that transforms the image of a simple cork bottle stopper. The work is focuses on the connection between glass a hard and compact material and cork, perfect porous material. The glass parts are done using free glass blowing. For the cork elements, sheets of agglomerated cork are used and milled using a CNC.

Archaic Nature

231

ROBERT STADLER

2008
Possible Furniture
Photography: André Morin
Producer: Galerie Emmanuel Perrotin Miami/Paris,
Robert Stadler

This unusual modular furniture set plays with our perception of balance and unbalance and thereby questions the designer's role in producing a "perfect" object. Each piece of furniture looks like an random pile but, on the contrary, is precisely designed following a standardardized set of rules dealing with ergonomics, stability and use.

KARIN AURAN FRANKENSTEIN

2009
1 **Cow Dung Lamp**
   Material: Clay, cow dung, sand,
   peet and paper
   Photography: Karin Auran Frankenstein

2008
2 **Cow Dung Shelf**
3 **Cow Dung Chair**
   Material: Clay, cow dung, sand,
   peet and paper
   Photography: Karin Auran Frankenstein

Old techniques are used in a new combination. Frankenstein has covered a welded structure with the dung mixture, molding some section and sculpting others.

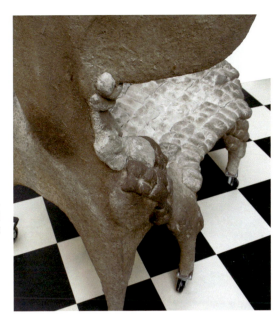

2

3

Shapeless — The New Ugly

1

AYALA SERFATY

2009
1 Anana Bench
Material: Fabric, bronze-finished brass,
buttons, down
Photography: Albi Serfaty

2009
2 Ears Stool
Material: Felt, metal
Photography: Albi Serfaty
Producer: Ears Stool

The first of a ground-breaking series of
three-dimensional hand-crafted felt upholstered pieces, the *Ears* stool proposes
innumerable options for custom design, using layered felt. The stool was created in collaboration with textile artist Irit Dulman

2

1

TTTVO

2005
1 **Dailyleftover Pillow**
   Material: Flex-foam, cow hide leather
   Producer: Studio Production

AYALA SERFATY

2009
2 **Gladis Lounge Armchair**
   Material: Fabric, polyurethane foam,
   swiveling ten-wheeled base
   Photography: Albi Serfaty
   Producer: Aqua Creations

2

ALON MERON

2008
1 The Aristocrats Easy Chair
Material: Wool, polysterene beads
Photography: Alon Meron
Producer: Alon Meron

These easy chairs are mongrels; part bean bag, part Chesterfield sofa – more casual than a Chesterfield, more supportive than a bean bag. Their special structure allows them to be supportive despite using only soft materials.

COM-PA-NY
Johan Olin

2005
2 Jesus Furniture
Material: Sofa, duct tape
Photography: Janne Suhonen
Producer: Com-pa-ny

Olin has rescued broken furniture using duct tape, also know as "Jesus tape."

1

2

BLOFIELD
Jeroen van de Kant

2009
1 Blofield Chair
Material: PVC, vinyl, air
Photography: Blofield
Producer: Blofield

A sofa filled with air that retains the looks and comfort of an authentic Chesterfield and meets the growing need for innovative and mobile (garden) furniture in a world where indoor and outdoor melt together.

ARIK BEN SIMHON

2009
2 Muscoli Easy Chair
3 Super Muscoli Easy Chair

Ben Simhon draws inspiration from the world of athletics with upholstery that references the protective padding used in hockey and skateboarding, as well as the polished tubular stainless steel structures used in gym equipment.ing the protective sportswear/pads used in hockey and skateboarding as well as polished tubular stainless steel structures inspired by gym equipment.

Shapeless — The New Ugly

ARIK BEN SIMHON

2009
1 Mickey Max Chaise Longue
2 Mickey Max Chaise Longue
3 Bambino Chair
4 Goldy Armchair

1

2

Hunting and Collecting
240

ONCE UPON A CHAIR

3

4

1

BRODIE NEILL

2009
1 @ Chair
  Material: Stainless steel
  Producer: Brodie Neill

STAFFAN HOLM DESIGN
Staffan Holm & Dan Sunaga

2009
2 Newton Coffee Table
  Material: Molded sheet wood
  Photography: Jonas Sällberg
  Producer: Karl Andersson & Söner

Newton's fascinating shape derives from the natural effect of the two rings' edges being forced towards the center using an ingenious method for cutting pressure-molded wood.

2

1

OSKAR ZIETA

2008/2009
1 FiDU Christmastree
Material: Thin metal sheets : ST3s
Photography: Oskar Zieta
Producer: Oskar Zieta

RONEN KADUSHIN

2006
2 Square Dance Coffee Table
Material: Lasercut stainless steel
Photography: Chanan Strauss
Producer: Open Design-Ronen Kadushin

Square Dance coffee table is a single piece of stainless steel that is bent by hand to an interlocking shape. It is an Open Design product, meaning, you can download the design, copy, modify and produce it under a Creative Commons license.

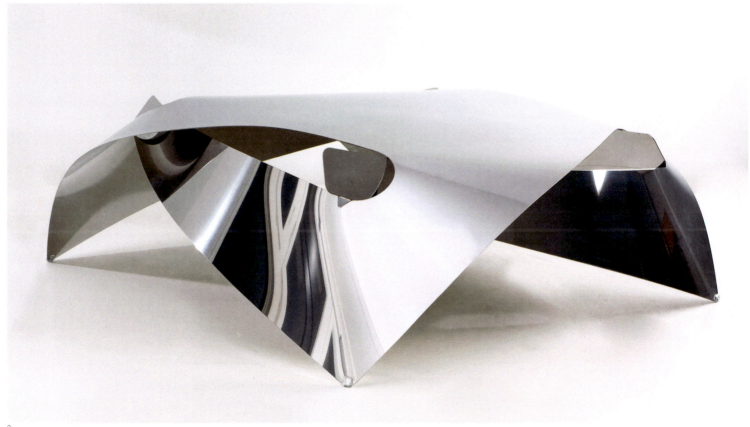

2

Soft – Edged
243

1

CÉDRIC RAGOT STUDIO

2007
1 Amibe Armchair and Stool
Material: Fibreglass
Photography: Cédric Ragot
Producer: L.A.M.F

Like a parasite, a mutant organism, taking revenge on industry.

JULIAN MAYOR

2009
2 Strata Chair
Material: Carbon fibre, fibreglass
Photography: Julian Mayor
Producer: Julian Mayor

CHRISTOFFER ANGELL

2008
3 Pauline Chaise Longue
Material: Plywood, Paul Smith pattern from Kvadrat
Photography: Jan Erik Svendsen

BRODIE NEILL

2008
4 Remix Bench
Material: Mixed plywoods, plastics
Photography: Andy Bird

2

3

4

1

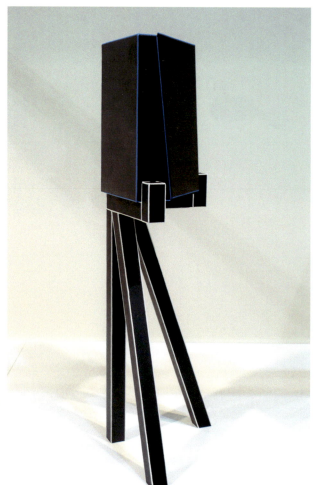

PHIL CUTTANCE

2009
1 **Weld Cabinet**
2 **Weld Table**
   Material: ABS plastic
   Photography: Phil Cuttance
   Producer: Phil Cuttance

The handcrafted *Weld* series utilises hot-air plastic welding, a process commonly used to repair broken plastic parts. This process is used to join thin plastic components and create strong, decorative edges. A departure from machine-made mass replicated plastic furniture, *Weld's* limited-edition pieces are each individually hand-crafted, idiosyncratic and therefore possess an inherent value unusual in plastic furniture.

2

KRÄUTLI
Florian Kräutli

2008
Animal Chairs
Material: Discarded steel frames,
foam, fake leather
Photography: Florian Kräutli

When you take off the skin of a cow, there's
the meat. When you take off the meat, you
have the skeleton. Kräutli's chairs are constructed like creatures, with skeletons, meat,
skin. The designer reassembles metal frames
found at the dump based on anatomic rules,
like an archeologist who discovers the bones
of a dinosaur.

1

PEPE HEYKOOP

2008
1 A Restless Chairacter
   Material: Aluminum, poyurethane rubber
   Photography: Lutz Sternstein
   Producer: Studio Pepe Heykoop

The inspiration for this chair came from an
old chair that loosened up over time. As the
years passed, it began to move and creak at
the joints. Heykoop captured this movement by replacing all its joints with rubber.
"On this chair you are allowed to lean back
on the legs," the designer says. "And even
with a book under one of the legs, the seat
wll level out."

KATHY LUDWIG

2008
2 Soft Wardrobe
   Material: Textile, Foam
   Photography: Florian Kräutli
   Producer: Unique piece

The *soft wardrobe* is supported and shaped
by the strength and volume of the items
stored inside. Its walls are not hard and supporting, rather they are soft like clothing. It
reacts in a particular way according to the
content with which the user fills it.

2

ONCE UPON A CHAIR

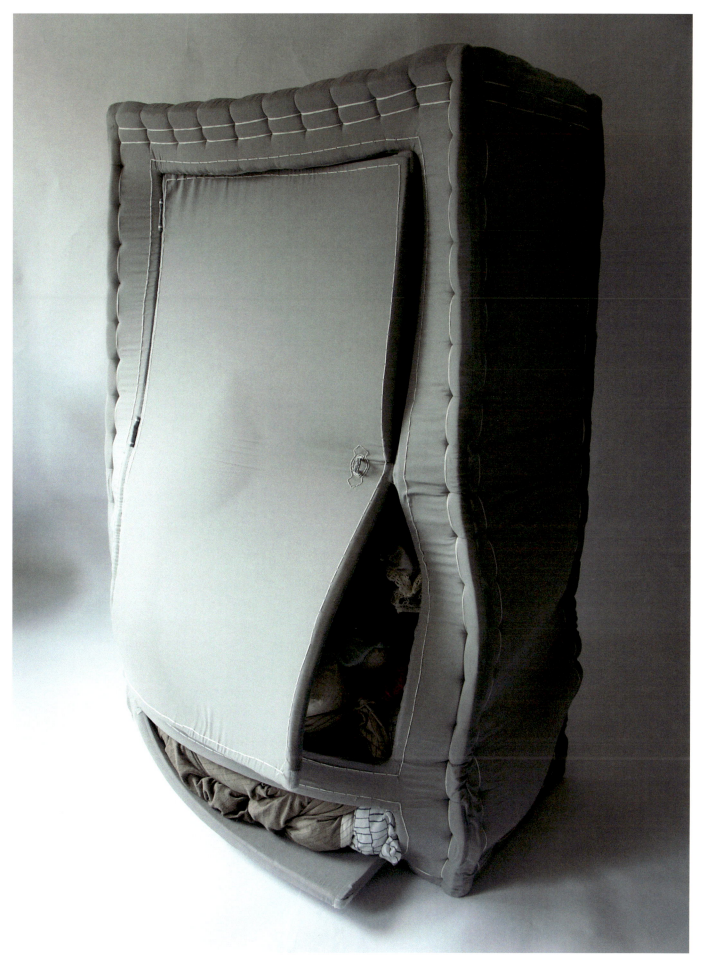

MATHIEU LEHANNEUR

2008
Bucky's Nightmare
Material: Leather
Photography: Fabien Thouvenin

In 1947, Buckminster Fuller represented science fiction translated into actual architecture when his geodesic dome was proven to be suitable for the construction of a wide range of stuctures. The blobby *Bucky's Nightmare*, in contrast with tensegrity, is a biomorphic leather island with a soft inside that re-configures geometrically under pressure, all the better to give support to each part of the human body.

BOUROULLEC BROTHERS
Ronan and Erwan Bouroullec

2008
Clouds Tiles
Material: Fabric, rubber bands
Photography: Paul Tahon, R & E Bouroullec
Producer: Kvadrat

Clouds is an innovative, interlocking fabric tile concept for the home. It can be used as an installation, hung from a wall or ceiling. *Clouds* tiles changes as units are added, using special rubber bands to attach them to each other, giving the structure depth and texture.

DESIGN RETHINK & DEVELOPMENT
Hannes Grebin

2008
1 **Ohrensessel Wing Chair**
   Material: Upholstery, wood, vintage fabric, doilies, fringe
2 **Deckenleuchte Pendant Lamp**
   Material: Glass, decor
3 **Perser "Persian" Rug**
   Material: Fabric
4 **Spiesser Sofa**
   Material: Upholstery, wood, vintage fabric, doilies, fringe
5 **Schrankwand Sideboard**
   Material: Wood
   Photography: Claudia Neuhaus

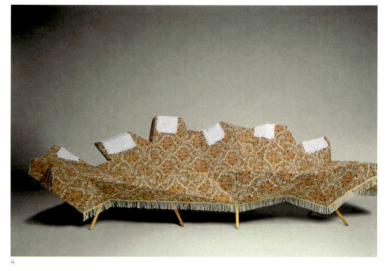

1

2009
1 An Unbalanced Table
   Material: Stainless steel
   Producer: Schinko GmbH

A table folded from polished sheet steel that, due to the method of folding, is self-supporting and requires no base. The table has a heavy side and a light side. It is not in balance.

2008
2 Filio Ring
   Material: Silver
   Producer: Thurner
3 A Viennese Pot (Teapot)
   Material: Silver
   Producer: Wiener Silberschmiede

1

2

3

CÉDRIC RAGOT STUDIO

2007
1 Tarmac Low Tables
Material: Fiberglass
Photography: Cédric Ragot
Producer: Roche Bobois

THOMAS FEICHTNER

2009
2 Pixel Chair
Material: Stainless steel
Producer: Schinko GmbH

Similar to the assembly and construction of car body parts in the automobile production process, *Pixel* is made stable through its strategic folding. The form of the back and armrests results from that of the legs, and vice-versa, so that every portion of the metal sheet serves a load-bearing function. Feichtner named the chair after Linz's Pixel Hotel, for which he designed a temporary hotel room filled with custom furniture inside a closed art gallery.

2008
3 Maya's Bed
Material: Wood
Producer: Holzwerkstatt Rehberger

1

2

3

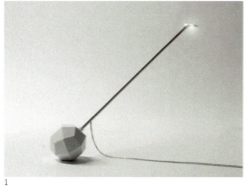

1

2

3

4

ARIHIRO MIYAKE

2009
1 **Carat Lamp**
Material: Brass,
powder-coated aluminum, LED
Photography: Studio Arihiro Miyake

CARROTHEAD

2008
2 **Around the Corner Shelving**
Material: MDF
Photography: Bernhard Moosbauer

STEPHAN VEIT

2007/2009
3 **Torno Side Table**
Material: Kunstquarz
Producer: Draenert

LEONHARD KLEIN

2008
4 **Laissez-Faire Light**
Material: Plexiglas®
Photography: Leonhard Klein

CECILIA LUNDGREN

2009
5 **Vika Coffee Table**
Material: Laquered aluminium

CHRISTIAN VIVANCO

2009
6 **Insitu Low Chair**
Material: Powder-coated steel, concrete

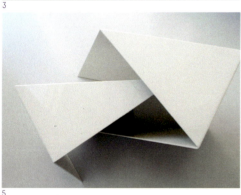

5

6

MICHAEL SCHONER

2006
1 **MLK Stool or Side Table**
  Photography: Michael Schoner
2 **MLK Stool or Side Table**
  Photography: Florent Le Corre
  Material: Alucobond

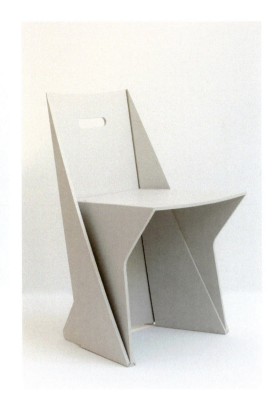

STUART MCFARLANE

2008
1 **Lapel Chair**
   Material: Recycled HDPE plastic
   Photography: Tony Owczarek
   Producer: Stuart McFarlane Industrial Design
2 **Lapel Chair**
   Photography: Stuart McFarlane

1

Lapel is a standard chair produced by folding 100% recycled plastic. This manipulation of material allows assembly in minutes without the use of glues or screws. In conjunction with a tool-less assembly, not only does it retrieve waste material from land fill, the designed outcome can be cleanly dismantled and re-recycled via domestic infrastructure. Inspired by origami folding techniques, *Lapel* is a sculpturally unique chair with outstanding environmental credentials. (*Lapel* is suitable for indoor and outdoor use and can hold weight up to 100kg.)

2

1

2

STUDIO LO

2009
1 Plic Shelf
Material: Cardboard
Photography: Studio Lo
Producer: Studio Lo

This folding corrugated cardboard shelf attaches to the wall using screws, plugs or even staples. Mounted in a few folds, it can support a load of 5 kg.

ALEXIS GEORGACOPOULOS

2008
2 Three-Legged Chair
Material: Steel

Georgacopoulos designed this chair, a work-in-progress, during a stay in Hong Kong, prototyping the piece in collaboration with local street trolley metalworkers.

Hard – Edged

SEBASTIAN JANSSON

2009
1 Habitus Stool
Material: Steel
Photography: Davide Bernardi

SERHAN GURKAN

2009
2 M2 Love Generation Coffee Table
Material: MDF
Photography: Kivanc Ince
Producer: Serhan Gurkan

AMPERSAND

2007
3 Wallpockets Organizers
Material: Corrugated cardboard
Photography: Davide Bernardi

Wallpockets was inspired by simple geometric shapes and the curious textures created by clusters of barnacles. They ship flat, and can be mounted to the wall using only tacks or adhesive strips. *Wallpockets* can also be placed over electrical outlets to create modern charging hubs that disguise messy cord-spaghetti.

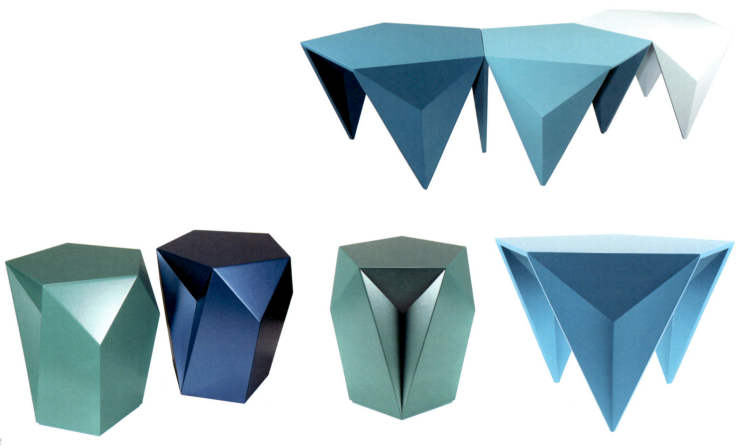

1

ADAM ROWE DESIGN

2008
1 **Victorian Grandfather Chair**
   Material: OSB, leather
   Photography: Johnny Kangasniemi
   Producer: Adam Rowe

First in a series of work challenging the misconceptions surrounding material aesthetics. Rowe combined traditional craftsmanship and high quality leather with a modern, cheap sustainable material, an OSB made from sustainable wood sources in the UK with no added formaldehyde..

RICHARD HUTTEN

1999-2007
2 **Playing with Tradition Rug**
   Material: Wool silk
   Producer: I+I

Hutten transforms the archetypal Persian carpet into a pattern of abstract contemporary stripes, as a reflection of modern, multicultural society.

PEPE HEYKOOP

2008
3 **Brickchair**
   Material: Wooden childrens'
   (building) bricks
   Photography: Pepe Heykoop
   Producer: Studio Pepe Heykoop

This chair represents Heykoop's response to a drawing made by James Gulliver Hancock, who once interpreted a chair into a childish drawing.

CHRISTIAN GIROUX & DANIEL YOUNG

2008
4 **Bonsai Art Work**
5 **Kermit Art Work**
6 **Mao Art Work**
   Material: Powder-coated Aluminum,
   Ikea furniture, components
   Photography: Peter Maccallum
   Producer: CGDY

2

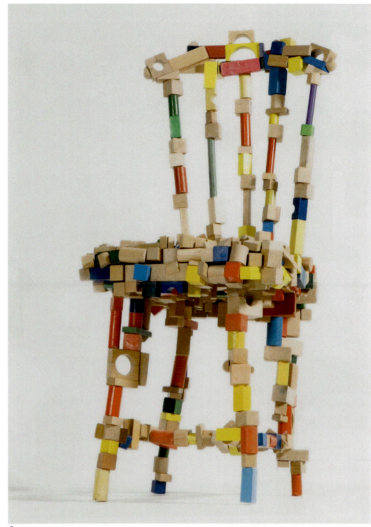

3

4

5

6

Pixel Park
265

Index

A

A.G. FRONZONI
www.cappellini.it
Page: 093

ADAM PATERSON
www.adampaterson.com
Page: 093

ADAM ROWE DESIGN
www.adamrowedesign.com
Page: 264

ADRIEN ROVERO
www.adrienrovero.com
Page: 075

ALAIN GILLES
www.alaingilles.com
Pages: 067, 167

ALEX HELLUM
www.alexhellum.com
Page: 155

ALEXIS GEORGACOPOULOS
www.georgacopoulos.com
Page: 261

ALISON BERGER GLASSWORKS
www.alisonbergerglassworks.com
Page: 052

ALON MERON
www.alonmeron.com
Pages: 103, 220, 238

AMPERSAND
www.ampersandbrand.com
Page: 263

ANTOINE + MANUEL
www.antoineetmanuel.com
Pages: 180, 181, 182

ARCHITETTURA ROCK
Niki Makariou
Su Hyun Lee
www.architetturarock.com
Pages: 103, 113

ARIHIRO MIYAKE
www.arihiromiyake.com
Pages: 134, 258

ARIK BEN SIMHON
www.arikbensimhon.com
Pages: 239, 240, 241

ARIK LEVY
www.ariklevy.fr
Pages: 052, 082, 083

ASIF KHAN
www.asif-khan.com
Page: 122

ASYMPTOTE
Hani Rashid & Lise-Anne Couture
www.asymptote.ne
Pages: 186, 187

ATELIER JACOB
Marco Jacob
www.atelierjacob.com
Page: 078

ATELIER NL
Nadine Sterk, Lonny van Ryswyck
www.ateliernl.com
Pages: 218, 219

AUTOBAN
Seyhan Özdemir & Sefer Çağlar
www.autoban212.com
Pages: 055, 195

AYALA SERFATY
www.aquagallery.com
Pages: 236, 237

B

BARBEROSGERBY
Edward Barber & Jay Osgerby
www.barberosgerby.com
Page: 187

BCXSY
www.bcxsy.com
Pages: 210, 211

BDDW
www.bddw.com
Pages: 222, 223

BENGTSSON DESIGN LTD
Mathias Bengtsson
www.bengtssondesign.com
Page: 078

BIG-GAME
Elric Petit, Augustin Scott de Martinville, Grégoire Jeanmonod
www.big-game.ch
Pages: 018, 169

BLA STATION
www.blastation.se
Page: 058

BLOFIELD
Jeroen van de Kant
www.blofield.com
Page: 239

BO REUDLER
www.boreudler.com
Pages: 156 - 157

BO YOUNG JUNG & EMMANUEL WOLFS
www.ammann-gallery.com
Page: 209

BOCA DO LOBO
Pedro Sousa
www.bocadolobo.com
Pages: 199, 200, 201

BOOKHOU
www.bookhou.com
Pages: 133, 206

BOUROULLEC BROTHERS
Ronan and Erwan Bouroullec
www.bouroullec.com
Pages: 066, 251, 252 – 253

BRAM BOO
www.bramboo.be
Pages: 094, 095

BRIKOLÖR
www.brikolor.com
Pages: 035, 164, 168, 174

BRODIE NEILL
www.brodieneill.com
Pages: 242, 245

BUBBLEUPROJECT
Kyung Sunghyun and Jeon Geehee
www.bubbleuproject.co
Page: 035

BYAMT INC
Alissia Melka-Teichroew
www.byamt.com
Page: 166

C

CARROTHEAD
www.carrothead.e
Page: 258

CASIMIRMEUBELEN
Casimir
www.casimirmeubelen.be
Pages: 026, 029

CATE&NELSON DESIGN
www.catenelson.com
Page: 032

Index

CECILIA LUNDGREN
www.ceciliadesign.s
Page: 258

CÉDRIC RAGOT STUDIO
www.cedricragot.com
Pages: 046, 244, 257

CHRISTIAN GIROUX
& DANIEL YOUNG
www.cgdy.co
Page: 265

CHRISTIAN HALLERÖD
Christian Halleröd and Johannes
Svartholm
www.chd.se
Pages: 090, 091

CHRISTIAN LESSING
www.christianlessing.de
Page: 111

CHRISTIAN VIVANCO
www.christianvivanco.com
Pages: 059, 110, 258

CHRISTOFFER ANGELL
www.christofferangell.com
Pages: 102, 245

CLAUDIO COLUCCI DESIGN
Claudio Colucci Design
Page: 166

COM-PA-NY
Johan Olin
www.com-pa-ny.com
Page: 238

D

DAG DESIGNLAB
www.dag-designlab.com
Page: 126

DANIEL ENOKSSON
www.danielenoksson.com
Page: 018

DANIEL LOVES OBJECTS
www.coroflot.com/daniellove
Page: 184

DANIEL ROHR
www.danielrohr.com
Page: 107

DECODE
t i m
decodelondon.com
Page: 222

DENNIS NINO CLASEN
www.clasen.tv
Pages: 020, 021

DESIGN RETHINK
& DEVELOPMENT
Hannes Grebin
www.grebin.de
Pages: 254, 255

DESIGNASYL
www.designasyl.blog.ch
Page: 108

DIANE STEVERLYNCK
www.dianesteverlynck.be
Page: 072

DITTE HAMMERSTROEM
www.hammerstroem.dk
Pages: 056, 057, 191

DRIFT
Lonneke Gordijn and Ralph Nauta
www.designdrift.nl
Page: 086

DUEESTUDIO
Claudia & Harry Washington
www.dueestudio.com
Pages: 025, 034, 178

DUNCAN BULL
Geoff Machen
www.duncanbull.co.uk
Pages: 053, 185

DUSTDELUXE
Damien Gernay
www.dustdeluxe.com
Page: 170

E

EDWARD VAN VLIET
www.sevv.com
Page: 061

ELISA STROZYK
www.elisastrozyk.de
Page: 135

ELLENBERGERDESIGN
STUDIO
Jannis Ellenberger
www.ellenbergerdesign.de
Page: 072

EMMEMOBILI
www.emmemobili.it
Pages: 174, 197

ERNESTO OROZA
www.oroza.net
Page: 080

F

FOLKFORM
www.folkform.se
Page: 150

FOR USE
For Use / Numen
www.foruse.eu
Page: 025

FORM US WITH LOVE
www.formuswithlove.se
Page: 019

FORMAFANTASMA
www.formafantasma.com
Pages: 146, 147

FORMFJORD
www.formfjord.com
Page: 019

FORMFORYOU
www.formforyou.se
Pages: 075, 167

FREDRIK FÄRG
www.fredrikfarg.com
Pages: 054, 055, 148

FREDRIK MATTSON
www.fredrikmattson.se
Pages: 019, 058, 114, 115

FREDRIKSON STALLARD
Patrik Fredrikson & Ian Stallard
www.fredriksonstallard.com
Pages: 129, 185, 207

FULGURO
Yves Fidalgo & Cédric Decroux
www.fulguro.ch
Page: 129

G

GAM PLUS FRATESI
GamFratesi
www.gamfratesi.com
Page: 081

GÄRSNÄS
www.garsnas.se
Pages: 055, 058

GITTA GSCHWENDTNER
www.gittagschwendtner.com
Page: 092

Index

GODSPEED
www.weareonlyinitforthemoney.com
Pages: 098, 099

GOLRAN SRL
www.golran.com
Page: 170

GREIGE
Daniel Lorch
www.daniellorch.de
Pages: 049, 075

H

HARCO RUTGERS
www.harcorutgers.nl
Page: 113

HARRI KOSKINEN WORKS
Harri Koskinen
www.harrikoskinen.com
Pages: 073, 085

HELLA JONGERIUS
www.jongeriuslab.com
Pages: 176, 177

HUMANS SINCE 1982
www.humanssince1982.com
Page: 163

HUNDREDS TENS UNITS
www.hundredstensunits.com
Page: 033

HUNN WAI
www.hunnwai.com
Pages: 104 – 105

I

IMAGINARY OFFICE
Daniel Hedner
www.imaginaryoffice.se
Pages: 042, 165

J

JACK BRANDSMA
www.jackbrandsma.com
Page: 110

JANG WON YOON
www.jangyoon.com
Page: 065

JARL FERNAEUS
www.jarlfernaeus.se
Page: 043

JARROD LIM DESIGN
Jarrod Lim
www.jarrodlim.com
Page: 084

JASON MILLER
www.millerstudio.us
Page: 211

JASON MILLER
www.millerstudio.us
Page: 211

JASPER MORRISON
www.cappellini.it
Pages: 069

JOHANNES HEMANN
www.johanneshemann.com
Pages: 130, 131

JONAS LYNDBY JENSEN
DESIGN
Jonas Lyndby Jensen
Morten la Cour
www.jonaslyndbyjensen.mdd.dk
Page: 055

JUDITH SENG
www.judithseng.de
Pages: 151, 168, 171

JULIAN MAYOR
www.julianmayor.com
Pages: 174, 244

K

KAI LINKE
www.kailinke.com
Page: 117

KAREN RYAN
www.bykarenryan.co.uk
Page: 101

KARIN AURAN FRANKENSTEIN
karin.frankenstein@gmail.com
Pages: 234, 235

KASPAR HAMACHER
www.kasparhamacher.be
Page: 031

KATHY LUDWIG
www.kathyludwig.com
Page: 248

KENSAKU OSHIRO
www.kensakuoshiro.com
Pages: 040, 161

KHAI LIEW
www.khailiew.com
Page: 173

KIKI VAN EIJK
www.kikiworld.nl
Page: 154

KILIAN SCHINDLER
www.kilianschindler.com
Page: 042

KONSTANTIN GRCIC
INDUSTRIAL DESIGN
Konstantin Grcic
www.konstantin-grcic.com
Page: 064

KORBAN / FLAUBERT
www.korbanflaubert.com.au
Page: 078

KRÄUTLI
Florian Kräutli
www.kraeutli.com
Pages: 032, 134, 247, 249

KRANEN / GILLE
www.kranengille.com
Page: 052

KWANGHO LEE
www.kwangholee.com
Pages: 126, 165

L

LAB::ISTANBUL
lab::istanbul
www.labistanbul.com
Page: 026

LABEL OBJET
www.labelobjet.com
Page: 191

LAURENT MASSALOUX
www.massaloux.net
Page: 129, 190

LEE BORTHWICK
www.leeborthwick.co.uk
Page: 230

Index

LELLO//ARNELL
Jørgen Craig Lello & Tobias Arnell
www.lelloarnell.com
Page: 192

LEONHARD KLEIN
www.leonhardklein.com
Page: 258

LIANA YAROSLAVSKY
www.lianayar.com
Page: 193

LIFEGOODS
www.lifegoods.ch
Page: 016

LLOT LLOV
www.llotllov.de
Pages: 108, 109, 111

LOGO STUDIO
Gean Moreno and Ernesto Oroza
www.oroza.net
Pages: 097

LORIS ET LIVIA
Loris Jaccard, Livia Lauber
www.lorisetlivia.com
Pages: 027, 040

LOUISE HINDSGAVL
www.danishcrafts.dk
Page: 197

LUKA STEPAN DESIGN
www.lukastepan.com
Pages: 124, 125

M

MAARTEN DE CEULAER
www.maartendeceulaer.com
Pages: 118, 161

**MAARTEN KOLK
& GUUS KUSTERS**
Maarten Kolk
www.mkgk.nl
Pages: 033, 149

MARC VENOT
www.marc-venot.com
Page: 053

MARCEL WANDERS STUDIO
www.marcelwanders.com
Pages: 060, 158, 159

MARCO DESSI
www.marcodessi.com
Page: 207

MARINA BAUTIER
www.lamaisondemarina.com
Pages: 030, 031

MARIO BOTTA
www.botta.ch
Pages: 226 – 227

MARK BRAUN
www.markbraun.org
Page: 230

MARK PRODUCT
Tom Raffield
www.markproduct.com
Page: 221

MARTÌ GUIXE
www.guixe.com
Page: 111

MARTIN BERGSTRÖM
www.martinbergstrom.com
Page: 149

MATALI CRASSET
www.matalicrasset.com
Page: 187

MATHIAS HAHN
www.mathiashahn.com
Pages: 018 ,053

MATHIAS VAN DE WALE
www.mathiasvandewalle.com
Page: 047

MATHIEU LEHANNEUR
www.mathieulehanneur.com
Page: 250

MAX LAMB
www.maxlamb.org
Pages: 096, 228, 229

MIA HAMBORG
www.miahamborg.com
Page: 115

MICHAEL SCHONER
www.michaelschoner.de
Pages: 113, 259

MILE
www.mileproject.jp
Page: 049

MISEWELL
Vincent and Paul Georgeson
www.misewell.com
Page: 020

MISO SOUP DESIGN
Daisuke Nagatomo & Minnie Jan
www.misosoupdesign.com
Pages: 044, 047

MOTOKI YOSHIO
www.yosh.io
Pages: 028, 230

MOUSTACHE
François Azambourg, Big-Game,
Matali Crasset, Ana Mir, Emili
Padros, Inga Sempé
www.moustache.fr
Pages: 038 – 039

N

NACH ACHT
www.nachacht.de
Page: 017

NACHO CARBONELL
www.nachocarbonell.com
Pages: 120, 121

NAOKI HIRAKOSO
www.hirakoso.jp
Page: 029

NENDO
Oki Sato
www.nendo.jp
Page: 160

NIKA ZUPANC
www.nikazupanc.com
Page: 059

NILS HOLGER MOORMANN
www.moormann.de
Page: 206

NOSIGNER
www.nosigner.com
Pages: 079, 221

O

OD-DO ARHITEKTI
www.od-do.com
Page: 109

OMER ARBEL
www.bocci.ca
Page: 179

ONZE STUDIO
www.onzestudio.com
Pages: 224, 225

Index

OSKAR ZIETA
www.zieta.pl
Page: 243

OSKO + DEICHMANN
www.oskodeichmann.com
Page: 080

OUT OF STOCK
www.outofstockdesign.com
Pages: 021, 035

P

PATRICIA URQUIOLA
www.patriciaurquiola.com
Pages: 060, 144, 145, 206

PATRICK BLANCHARD
www.madebymeta.com
Page: 188

PATRICK NORGUET
www.patricknorguet.com
Page: 069

PELIDESIGN
Alexander Pelikan
www.pelidesign.com
Pages: 022, 023

PEPE HEYKOOP
www.pepeheykoop.nl
Pages: 124, 172, 248, 265

PETER ANDERSSON
www.peterandersson.com
Page: 103

PETER MACAPIA
labdora.com
Page: 123

PETER MARIGOLD
www.libbysellers.com
Page: 208

PETER SCHÄFER
www.peterschaefer.net
Page: 106

PETTER SKOGSTAD
www.petterskogstad.com
Page: 063

PHIL CUTTANCE
www.philcuttance.com
Page: 246

PHILIP MICHAEL WOLFSON
www.wolfsondesign.com
Page: 054

PHILIPPE BESTENHEIDER
www.bestenheider.com
Pages: 041, 061, 185, 198, 199

PHILIPPE NIGRO
www.philippenigro.com
Page: 072

PIERO LISSONI
Piero Lissoni for Porro
www.porro.com
Page: 027

PIERRE KRACHT
www.pierrekracht.de
Pages: 162, 163

PIET BOON ZONE
www.pietboonzone.nl
Page: 197

POSTFOSSIL
Anna Blattert & Daniel Gafner
Thomas Walde
Claudia Heiniger
Florian Hauswirth
Christine Birkhoven
www.postfossil.ch
Pages: 216, 217

POUR LES ALPES
Annina Gähwiler & Tina Stieger
www.pourlesalpes.ch
Page: 153

PUNGA AND SMITH
www.pungaandsmith.com
Pages: 045, 111, 129, 179

R

RAIMUND PUTS
www.moooi.com
Page: 084

RAW-EDGES
Yael Mer & Shay Alkalay
www.raw-edges.com
Pages: 128

REDDISH STUDIO
Naama Steinbock & Idan Friedman
www.reddishstudio.com
Pages: 122, 151, 171

REINHARD DIENES
www.reinharddienes.com
Pages: 025, 065

RICHARD HUTTEN
www.richardhutten.com
Pages: 127, 265

RIJADA
Rihards Funts, Peteris Buks
www.rijada.lv
Pages: 231

ROBERT STADLER
www.robertstadler.net
Pages: 232 – 233

RONEN KADUSHIN
www.ronen-kadushin.com
Pages: 125, 243

RYAN DART DESIGN
www.ryandartdesign.com
Pages: 062, 175

S

SAM BARON
Valentina Carretta for Fabrica
www.sambaron.blogspot.com
Page: 220

SAMARE
Laurie and Mania Bedikian,
Nicolas Bellavance-Lecompte,
Patrick Meirim de Barros
www.samare.ca
Page: 067

SANDER MULDER
www.sandermulder.com
Page: 048

SATYENDRA PAKHALÉ
www.ammann-gallery.com
Page: 194

SCHEMA ARCHITECTURE
OFFICE
Jo Nagasaka
www.eandy.com
Page: 112

SCOTT GARCIA
www.scottgarcia.moonfruit.com
Page: 207

SCOTT JARVIE
www.scottjarvie.co.uk
Page: 132

SCRAP LAB
www.scraplab.org
Page: 133

SEBASTIAN BRAJKOVIC
www.sebastianbrajkovic.com
Pages: 116, 195

SEBASTIAN ERRAZURIZ
www.meetsebastian.com
Page: 024

Index

SEBASTIAN HERKNER
www.sebastianherkner.com
Pages: 050, 051

SEBASTIAN JANSSON
www.sebastianjansson.com
Page: 262

SEMIGOOD DESIGN
Thom Jones
www.semigoods.com
Page: 034

SERHAN GURKAN
www.serhangurkan.com
Pages: 068, 262

SHI JIANMIN
www.ammann-gallery.com
Page: 194

SHIGE HASEGAWA
www.shige-hasegawa.com
Page: 048

SHIGERU BAN
www.shigerubanarchitects.com
Pages: 070, 071

SIBYLLE STŒCKLI
www.sibyllestoeckli.com
Pages: 100, 119

SNODEVORMGEVERS
Mander Liefting & Josef Blersch
www.snodevormgevers.nl
Page: 152

STAFFAN HOLM DESIGN
Staffan Holm & Dan Sunaga
www.staffanholm.com
Page: 242

STEFAN DIEZ
www.stefan-diez.com
Pages: 036, 037

STEPHAN VEIT
www.stephanveit.com
Pages: 230, 258

STOKKEAUSTAD
www.stokkeaustad.com
Page: 054

STONE DESIGN
www.stone-dsgns.com
Page: 073

STUART MCFARLANE
www.stuartmcfarlane.com
Page: 260

STUDIO BILITY
Gudrun Lilja & Jon Asgeir
www.bility.is
Page: 030

STUDIO DROR
Dror Benshetrit
www.studiodror.com
Page: 040

STUDIO GORM
www.studiogorm.com
Pages: 042, 043

STUDIO JO MEESTERS
www.jomeesters.nl
Pages: 150, 214, 215

STUDIO JOB
Job Smeets + Nynke Tynagel
www.studiojob.be
Pages: 140,141, 142, 143, 196

STUDIO LO
www.studiolodesign.fr
Pages: 220, 261

STUDIO MAKKINK & BEY
Rianne Makkink & Jurgen Bey
www.jurgenbey.nl
Page: 074, 212, 213

STUDIO NIELS & SVEN
www.nielsensven.nl
Page: 209

T

TAKESHI MIYAKAWA DESIGN
www.tmiyakawadesign.com
Pages: 024, 045, 172, 173

THE GREEN HOUSE
ARCHITECTS
Niklas Madsen/Per Eriksson
thegreenhouseark.wordpress.com
Page: 107

THOMAS FEICHTNER
www.thomasfeichtner.com
Pages: 256, 257

TIAGO DA FONSECA
www.tiagodafonseca.com
Page: 183

TINA ROEDER
Tina Roeder & David Krings
www.tinaroeder.com
Page: 175

TOKUJIN YOSHIOKA
www.tokujin.com
Pages: 063, 075, 127

TOM DE VRIEZE
www.tovdesign.com
Page: 208

TOM DIXON
www.tomdixon.net
Pages: 076, 077

TOM PRICE
www.tom-price.com
Page: 111

TOMÁS ALONSO
www.tomas-alonso.com
Page: 016

TOMAS KRAL
www.tomaskral.ch
Page: 231

TOMITADESIGN
Kazuhiko Tomita
www.tomitadesign.com
Page: 049

TORD BOONTJE
www.tordboontje.com
Pages: 149, 188, 189

TTTVO
www.tttvo.nl
Page: 237

V

VALENTINA GONZALEZ
WOHLERS
www.valentinagw.com
Page: 119

W

WARM & STOLZENBURG
Corinna Warm
www.warmandstolzenburg.com
Pages: 069

Z

ZOË MOWAT
www.zoemowat.com
Page: 109

Edited by Robert Klanten, Sven Ehmann, Andrej Kupetz & Shonquis Moreno
Cover and layout by Floyd Schulze for Gestalten
Preface and chapter introductions by Andrej Kupetz
Project descriptions by Shonquis Moreno for Gestalten
Typefaces: SangBleu BP by Ian Party, Foundry: B&P (www.bpfoundry.com)
T-Star by Michael Mischler, Foundry: Gestalten (www.gestalten.com/fonts)

Project management by Elisabeth Honerla for Gestalten
Production management by Janine Milstrey for Gestalten
Proofreading by Joseph Pearson
Printed in Hong Kong through Asia Pacific Offset

Published by Gestalten, Berlin 2009
ISBN 978-3-89955-256-0

For more information, please check www.gestalten.com

Bibliographic information published by the Deutsche Nationalbibliothek.
The Deutsche Nationalbibliothek lists this publication in the Deutsche Nationalbibliografie;
detailed bibliographic data is available on the internet at http://dnb.d-nb.de.

None of the content in this book was published in exchange for payment by commercial
parties or designers; Gestalten selected all included work based solely on its artistic merit.

Gestalten is a climate neutral company and so are our products. We collaborate with the non-
profit carbon offset provider myclimate (www.myclimate.org) to neutralize the company's
carbon footprint produced through our worldwide business activities by investing in projects
that reduce CO_2 emissions (www.gestalten.com/myclimate).